Of Medicines and Markets

T0305342

Stanford Studies in Human Rights

Of Medicines and Markets

*Intellectual Property and Human
Rights in the Free Trade Era*

Angelina Snodgrass Godoy

Stanford University Press
Stanford, California

Stanford University Press
Stanford, California

© 2013 by the Board of Trustees of the Leland Stanford Junior University.
Printed and bound by CPI Group (UK) Ltd, Croydon, CR0 4YY

Library of Congress Cataloging-in-Publication Data
Godoy, Angelina Snodgrass, author.

Of medicines and markets : intellectual property and human rights in the free trade era / Angelina Snodgrass Godoy.

pages cm. — (Stanford studies in human rights)
Includes bibliographical references and index.
ISBN 978-0-8047-8560-0 (cloth : alk. paper) — ISBN 978-0-8047-8561-7 (pbk. : alk. paper)

1. Drug accessibility—Central America. 2. Pharmaceutical policy—Central America. 3. Right to health—Central America. 4. Intellectual property—Central America. 5. Drugs—Patents. 6. Free trade—Central America. 7. Human rights—Central America. I. Title. II. Series: Stanford studies in human rights.

RA401.C35G63 2013
338.4'7615109728—dc23

2012043945

Typeset by Thompson Type in 10/14 Minion

Contents

Foreword

AS SHE EXPLAINS, Angelina Snodgrass Godoy first took notice of the coming conflicts around human rights, intellectual property, and the demands of global free trade regimes during a research trip to Guatemala, a country that was slowly emerging from the social ravages of a decades-long civil war and the horrors of a genocide committed against its indigenous populations. As the process of postconflict reconciliation and accounting matured, albeit unevenly and without resolution, the coalitions of local and transnational human rights networks that had coalesced around demands for justice broke apart, the topic of the genocide itself disappeared from national newspapers, and the country retreated into its more mundane struggles with poverty, development, and political transition. But, at the same time, Guatemala, like other countries in Central America, was negotiating the terms of the Central American Free Trade Agreement, the regional version of the earlier NAFTA that had brought Canada, the United States, and Mexico together into a controversial free trade zone. Although Guatemalan human rights activists were not focused initially on CAFTA, they soon realized that the terms of the agreement, especially around intellectual property, threatened the human rights of Guatemalans in more subtle ways. These included the deeply ingrained right to health, because a key provision of CAFTA outlined strong intellectual property protections that would make it more difficult for poor countries like Guatemala to produce cheaper generic drugs that were affordable and locally available.

Some of these drugs represented the difference between life and death for people, including the antiretrovirals that are used to treat patients with HIV. Godoy observed as the serious implications of CAFTA for people in Guatemala soon dawned on patients, government workers, and human rights activists. What she was witnessing was the emergence of new threats to human rights that did not have the same immediacy and sense of urgency as the kind of massive physical integrity violations that had provoked transnational outrage and had made Guatemala one of the icons of injustice within the international human rights movement. Instead, the looming consequences of CAFTA represented something quite different and, in some ways, farther reaching: a clash between the imperatives of global capital and the imperatives of human rights in countries that had been at the forefront of human rights ratification and promotion, especially after the end of the Cold War.

Godoy decided to study this clash more systematically, and this book is the result. She broadened her empirical focus to include El Salvador and Costa Rica, and the sweep of her analytical frame came to encompass one of the most important questions of our time: whether contemporary human rights and the dominant modes of global freed trade represent fundamentally contradictory approaches to world making and social ordering. *Of Medicines and Markets* uses the struggle to ensure health rights in three Central American countries in the face of pressures to preserve the profit margins of giant, mostly North American, pharmaceutical companies, to reflect more generally on the changing nature of human rights activism, the role of the state, and the ways in which demands for social justice can face implacable structural barriers in smaller countries that lack relative bargaining power in broader political economies. Her book is also a powerful reminder that new struggles for human rights have become difficult to recognize in many cases. As she puts it:

> While the iconic figure in decades past was the prisoner of conscience, the courageous dissident imprisoned for daring to speak his mind, today's struggles feature new actors: indigenous people opposing the construction of dams on their ancestral lands; factory workers rallying against the "cut and run" practices of transnational capital; AIDS patients demanding affordable drugs from an industry whose pricing places the pills beyond their grasp.

In the process of revealing for us the landscapes of these new terrains on which human rights activists must now do their work, Godoy gives us a landmark critical history of the right to health in Central America, which is a key marker of the way in which Latin America more generally has long been a region at the forefront of the postwar development of human rights. Through her empirical study and history of the right to health in Central America, and her analysis of the key role that intellectual property regimes play in complicating this right, she confronts the central problem of human rights promotion in a world shaped by the imperatives of capital. Her reflections on this problem provide a new conceptual model for understanding the practice of human rights and redirect our focus on the form and content of future human rights struggles that are just over the horizon.

Mark Goodale
Series Editor

Acronyms and Abbreviations

ACAM   Alianza Civil por el Acceso a Medicamentos, a coalition
              of Guatemalan civil society organizations opposed to
              increased IP protections

ASINFARGUA   Association of Guatemalan Pharmaceutical Industry
              (*Asociación de Industriales Farmacéuticos Guatemalte-
              cos*), a trade group representing the interests of leading
              generic pharmaceutical producers in Guatemala

CAFTA   United States-Central America Free Trade Agreement,
              also known as DR-CAFTA, United States-Dominican
              Republic-Central America Free Trade Agreement

Caja   Costa Rican Social Security Institute (*Caja Costarri-
              cense de Seguridad Social*)

FEDEFARMA   Central American Federation of Pharmaceutical
              Laboratories (*Federación Centroamericana de Labora-
              torios Farmacéuticos*), an organization representing the
              interest of transnational pharmaceutical companies in
              Central America, including the originator companies
              associated with PhRMA

GAO   U.S. Government Accounting Office

IDB   Inter-American Development Bank

IGSS   Guatemalan Social Security Institute (*Instituto Guate-
              malteco de Seguridad Social*)

IMF   International Monetary Fund

INQUIFAR	Association of Salvadoran Pharmaceutical Industry (*Asociación de Industriales Químico Farmacéuticos de El Salvador*), a trade group representing the interests of leading generic pharmaceutical producers in El Salvador
IP	intellectual property
IPR	intellectual property rights
ISSS	Salvadoran Social Security Institute (*Instituto Salvadoreño de Seguridad Social*)
PAHO	Pan-American Health Organization
PDH	Human Rights Ombudsman's Office (*Procuraduría de Derechos Humanos*), an institution of the legislative branch in Guatemala and El Salvador (the equivalent in Costa Rica is known as the *Defensoría de los Habitantes*)
PhRMA	Pharmaceutical Research and Manufacturers of America (colloquially referred to as "Big Pharma"), an organization representing the major pharmaceutical companies
TRIPS	WTO's Agreement on Trade-Related Aspects of Intellectual Property Rights, 1994
UNICEF	UN Fund for Children
US FDA	U.S. Food and Drug Administration
WHO	World Health Organization
WTO	World Trade Organization

Acknowledgments

I AM DEEPLY INDEBTED to many people who have assisted me in the multi-year process of researching and writing this book. First and foremost, I am very grateful to my informants and collaborators—especially those Central Americans who took time out of their busy schedules to help me understand the dynamics of intellectual property and access to medicines from their vantage point. There are too many such people to name all individually, and some preferred that their participation be anonymous, but all helped me make sense of this complex panorama, and without their generosity and insights this book would simply never have been possible to write.

Over the years I have collaborated with various scholars and scholar-practitioners working on intellectual property issues. In particular, I want to acknowledge my immense gratitude and respect for my close collaborator and friend Alejandro Cerón. I also learned tremendously from my contact with the members of the CEPIAM Network: from Costa Rica, Luis Bernardo Villalobos Solano, Gabriela Arguedas Ramírez, and Victoria Hall; from El Salvador, Eduardo Espinoza Fiallos, Giovanni Guevara Vásquez, and María Angela Elías Marroquín; from Guatemala, Alfredo Moreno and César García; from Honduras, Edna Janeth Maradiaga Martínez and Jorge Sierra; and from Nicaragua, Carlos Berríos and Douglas Quintero. And I have also been greatly enriched by my relationship with a cadre of scholars probing related issues in the Colombian context, including César Rodríguez-Garavito, Diana Rodríguez Franco, and Tatiana Andia.

I am also fortunate to have relied on a range of colleagues and friends in human rights and law and society circles for feedback as this manuscript took shape. Michael McCann, in particular, has been exorbitantly generous in reading multiple drafts of this work over the years and always providing thoughtful, incisive commentary that has sharpened the final product considerably. My colleagues Jamie Mayerfeld and Glenda Pearson also read chapter drafts and provided feedback, as did David Gartner. I also benefited greatly from the opportunity to share excerpts from this work in other settings, including the LSJ/CLASS Workshare at the University of Washington, the Colloquium on Innovation Policy at NYU, the Universidad de Costa Rica, and the Universidad de los Andes in Colombia. I particularly appreciate the thoughtful feedback provided by Rochelle Dreyfuss, César Rodríguez-Garavito, and Peter Evans in these encounters.

Lastly, my perspectives and thinking have benefited from numerous exchanges with practitioners in this field, including especially Judit Rius Sanjuán and Rohit Malpani. I am greatly indebted to Carmen Pérez of INQUIFAR in El Salvador and to the many pharmaceutical company executives who shared their views with me in all three countries examined in these pages. Karen Vargas served as a particularly helpful friend, advisor, and source of inspiration over the course of my multiple visits to Costa Rica in recent years. In El Salvador, I am also particularly grateful to Rolando González, whose generosity of spirit and practical assistance helped me grapple with the complexities of his small but beautiful country throughout the years I worked on this book.

At Stanford University Press, I've been fortunate to work with Mark Goodale, Kate Wahl, and Frances Malcolm; their contributions to this manuscript have also been considerable and much appreciated. Similarly, Margaret Pinette's precise attention to every detail has greatly improved this work.

This work would also not have been possible without the generous support of numerous organizations. I'm grateful for financial support received from the Puget Sound Partners for Global Health, as well as American Council of Learned Societies and the Ford Foundation. I also benefited from funding provided by the National Science Foundation through Grant No. 0617374 and from the generosity of the Henry M. Jackson Foundation in establishing the Helen H. Jackson Chair in Human Rights, which I currently hold at the University of Washington.

Lastly, to my family, and most especially Estuardo, I owe infinitely more than can be expressed in words; thank you.

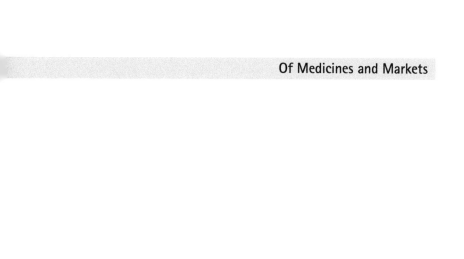

Of Medicines and Markets

Chapter 1

Trading Health for Wealth

E DGAR'S SMILE WAS NOT A POLITE nice-to-meet you smirk but one of those grins that first ignited in his coffee-colored eyes and then radiated, broad and beautiful, across his face. He settled into his plastic chair and leaned forward, friendly, engaged, eager to hear the questions we'd come to ask him. Among an organization of strikingly optimistic people, Edgar seemed particularly so. Yet, cast against his unassailably generous spirit, the one question he asked us was devastating: "Why would your Congress make it harder for me to get my medicine?"

My students and I met Edgar in the summer of 2004, in the offices of a Guatemalan HIV+ organization called Gente Positiva. At that time, CAFTA—the U.S.–Central America Free Trade Agreement—was awaiting ratification in all the member countries. The agreement was the first major extension of the NAFTA (North American Free Trade Agreement) model, hailed as a stepping-stone to an eventual Free Trade Area of the Americas; its announcement had touched off battles around labor rights, environmental protection, and threats to peasant agriculture. In addition, critics had begun to raise concerns about the agreement's chapter 15, which governed intellectual property (IP) rights. In Guatemala in particular, a coalition of public health, human rights, and alter-globalization activists had come together to advocate against the IP provisions in CAFTA, which they argued would curtail access to medicines by limiting the availability of low-cost generics. On the day the Guatemalan Congress ratified the agreement, some took to the streets wearing jerseys emblazoned with the slogan, "My life is not for sale." This was a new issue for Central American human rights advocates. Indeed, CAFTA itself was something of a turning point for the movement, marking a new era of engagement with global economic structures.

Guatemala, like some other countries of the region, had only recently emerged from a prolonged armed conflict that had inflicted deep and painful wounds on the social fabric; a UN Truth Commission had declared in 1999 that the atrocities committed in the context of the thirty-six-year war constituted a genocide against the indigenous Maya. When I began research on human rights issues in Guatemala in the mid-1990s, the field was dominated by discussions of postwar justice and reconciliation. Forensic anthropologists spearheaded the scientific exhumations of mass graves littered across the countryside; lawyers undertook the careful work of knitting together testimonies with legal tools, seeking accountability for wartime atrocities; the UN Mission in Guatemala, tasked with verifying compliance with the Peace Accords, issued periodic reports on the status of implementation efforts; human rights organizations documented threats against witnesses in court cases and called for truth telling about past violence. Everywhere, the focus was on issues related to state violence.

But by 2004, when we met Edgar, things had shifted perceptibly. Donor support for the various legal accountability efforts had waned, perhaps in response to disheartening outcomes—even today, the military leaders responsible for crimes against humanity have largely eluded justice—or perhaps in reflection of a broader reframing of global human rights concerns in the wake of 9/11. The UN Mission had left the country. Various forms of international assistance were still present, but they tended increasingly to place priority on alleviating the region's enduring poverty rather than promoting postwar justice. The genocide had mostly slipped from the headlines. In this context, beginning in 2003, behind closed doors and without any involvement from civil society organizations, the governments of the United States and various Central American countries—Costa Rica, El Salvador, Guatemala, Honduras, and Nicaragua—had hammered out a comprehensive agreement that established new rules and procedures for trade relations.

If some in the human rights community had until then considered trade law a technical province of administrative procedures largely unrelated to its core concerns with justice and accountability, such assumptions faded fast when CAFTA's content was unveiled in 2004. Amid the layers of legalese were new rules for doing business across borders; new limits on what national laws could regulate, promote, or prohibit vis-à-vis the conduct of private industry; new institutions for adjudicating disputes between corporations and governments; and new ways of envisioning the social contract.

Given the history of Central America, it was not difficult to imagine that these ways of reconfiguring corporate relationships with states in an interdependent global arena could have human rights implications. This was nowhere clearer than in Guatemala, once the proverbial "banana republic" where an attempt to nationalize lands held by a U.S. corporation—United Fruit, now known as Chiquita—had triggered the ouster of democratically elected President Jacobo Arbenz in a 1954 coup backed by the CIA (Central Intelligence Agency). The violence that followed the coup rapidly devolved into civil war, as a series of U.S.-backed dictators took turns battling Marxist guerrillas and eventually waging genocide against the country's indigenous majority. So, some seven years after the signing of the country's Peace Accords, when the text of CAFTA was made public, those paying attention immediately recognized what was at stake and scrambled to organize in response.

But it was an uphill battle: Prolonged civil wars had turned societies inward, had polarized them along ideological lines, and had decimated civic engagement. The issues in the agreement were complex and cloaked in language that was difficult to understand. And poverty, the lack of education, and underemployment already had the majority of the region's population locked in a daily struggle for subsistence, in which informing themselves on the finer points of trade law, let alone manning the barricades, seemed a tall order. While progressive unions, peasant groups, and—to a lesser extent—environmental organizations rallied their bases to oppose relevant chapters in the agreement, there *was* no preexisting Central American advocacy group dealing with intellectual property. The issue was brand new.

During the CAFTA ratification process, I sought in my own limited way to contribute a human rights voice to the intellectual property discussion through opinion pieces, meetings with congresspeople, and general advocacy. In one of those discussions, when my students and I shared our work with our congressman before a research trip to Guatemala, he advised us to meet with people who'd be affected by CAFTA's IP chapter while there and to note their stories, even take their pictures so as to later be able to personify the harm this legislation would bring. Following his advice, we went to the offices of Gente Positiva to meet some of the HIV+ patients who the organization was concerned might lose access to antiretroviral drugs under the terms of the agreement's more restrictive intellectual property laws. Edgar was one of several HIV+ patients kind enough to share his story with us that July day.

I always tell my students to be mindful of the ethics of interviewing and to give the interviewee a chance to turn the tables and pose questions, too; it's only fair, after all, if we are asking them to open their lives to us, that we might be expected to do the same in return. So after an engaging, pleasant conversation with Edgar in which we mainly discussed his experiences living with HIV and his challenges obtaining the antiretroviral drugs he needed to stay alive, we asked him if he had any questions for us.

"Yes," he said, smiling, as he had throughout our time together. He paused slightly to gather his thoughts. "Why would your Congress make it harder for me to get my medicine?"

This was the question that I found devastating. I stammered something about the agreement's complexity and voters' ignorance, but a real answer would have had something to do with the agreement's unstated premise that certain lives were expendable, and I didn't have the courage to say that. He smiled—again—and graciously let it go. But in that moment I made a silent commitment to share his story and that of other Central Americans whose access to drugs was challenged by U.S. trade policy.

Why Intellectual Property Matters

The intellectual property debate should matter to us, I believe, on at least two levels. First and most directly, IP affects who gets access to medicine—including, in cases like Edgar's, medicine that marks the difference between life and death. If we care about human rights, we need to understand how these policies work and the impacts they have on real people's lives. Those of us who are Americans have a particular duty to do so, as these policies are promoted in our name, using our tax dollars.

Secondly, however, intellectual property should also matter on another level to those of us concerned with human rights. We know human rights tactics can work—within limits—against the violation of civil and political rights by authoritarian governments. Amnesty International cut its teeth contesting the torture and imprisonment of political opponents in the 1970s Southern Cone; Human Rights Watch began as Helsinki Watch, scrutinizing and denouncing abuses behind the Iron Curtain. Decades later, a vast and vibrant field of interdisciplinary scholarship in human rights has examined when and how such tactics have proved effective at reining in repression through appeals to international norms.

Yet today's human rights headlines increasingly call attention to new challenges. While the iconic figure in decades past was the prisoner of conscience, the courageous dissident imprisoned for daring to speak his mind, today's struggles feature new actors: indigenous people opposing the construction of dams on their ancestral lands; factory workers rallying against the "cut and run" practices of transnational capital; AIDS patients demanding affordable drugs from an industry whose pricing places the pills beyond their grasp. In these and other cases, the international legal order is not always an antidote to abuses; some rights violations stem from transnational structures, and some violators even justify their actions by citing international trade law. Particularly as regards social and economic rights, sometimes the challenge requires empowering a reticent state rather than restraining a repressive one. In this context, how potent are the concepts and tools of human rights at prompting counterhegemonic transformations? Are transnational human rights capable of challenging global economic dictates, or do they merely provide a fig leaf for contemporary forms of exploitation?

I believe the struggles over intellectual property and access provide a uniquely propitious site for examining this question. For although there are numerous points of friction between human rights and international commercial law, IP represents the site of clearest contradiction between these two ways of ordering our world. The way in which this conflict in perspectives is resolved, then, bears broad relevance to a host of contemporary struggles over rights, justice, and the role of the market in social life.

Why Central America Matters

Central America makes for a particularly apt site from which to examine the frictions between intellectual property and human rights, for three reasons. First, CAFTA represents the largest trade agreement to date to include "TRIPS-plus" IP provisions, a term that refers to standards exceeding those established under TRIPS (the 1994 Agreement on Trade-Related Aspects of Intellectual Property Rights, the global agreement establishing a single universal set of IP standards for all WTO [World Trade Organization] member nations). What's more, the IP standards in CAFTA are, on balance, more demanding than those contained in bilateral trade agreements that preceded it *and* in agreements that followed it.[1] This means that, at this point, CAFTA's standards represent the global high-water mark in intellectual property protection.

Second, the right to health enjoys a relatively high degree of constitutional protection in the countries of Central America. A recent study found that 90 percent of court cases worldwide in which the right to health was invoked to seek access to medications came from Central and South America, suggesting that those seeking to advance legislative or judicial frameworks that prioritize to the right to health might enjoy some advantages in this region (Hogerzeil et al. 2006, 305). In this sense, the CAFTA countries find themselves situated on the front lines of this debate; how they navigate these competing pressures may contain lessons for other parts of the world.

And third, it is important to examine the impact of intellectual property policy in a diversity of national and regional settings. While the years since TRIPS have seen important public health victories, not all of these can be broadly generalized; the attention they have generated may yield mistaken assumptions about what policy options are possible. For example, the bold stance of Brazil, a country that has repeatedly granted compulsory licenses to allow the domestic production of generics, is made possible by the country's status as an economic powerhouse and the considerable capacity of its domestic pharmaceutical sector—advantages most developing countries lack (Shadlen 2009). The high-profile campaign of South African HIV+ patients and their transnational allies, similarly, was successful in forcing the United States to withdraw its suit against their government for allowing the production of generic antiretrovirals, but not all countries or diseases command such sympathy in the court of public opinion (or, for that matter, in any court). And while the coalition building among Global South countries at the WTO made possible the landmark Doha declaration, which lays out key flexibilities in IP rules that states can invoke to protect public health, in recent years the most aggressive forms of IP lawmaking have taken the form of bilateral trade agreements struck between the United States or EU (European Union) and much less powerful nations. The negotiating climate in such deals makes it much more difficult for weaker countries to secure human rights concessions. For all of these reasons, then, it is important to investigate the implications of intellectual property policy for the right to health in relatively smaller nations, which confront strong IP pressures yet may not enjoy the same policy making (or politics making) possibilities as trailblazers like Thailand and Brazil.

Research Design

When I embarked on this research project, I was driven by two related research questions. The first was an empirical one: I wanted to know what CAFTA's impact would be in Central America, and I was concerned that it seemed there was little interest in rigorous research on this point. In brief, I thought that by conducting some of this research myself I might actually make a difference. And second, I was interested in a broader theoretical question: Will the tools of human rights be effective against threats arising from the global economic order? Or, to put it differently, even if we could determine with scientific precision what CAFTA's impact on health would be, could we really do anything about it?

I began my work by tackling the empirical heavy lifting. I started out by working to predict the agreement's impact by analyzing its implementation legislation across all six CAFTA countries, including the Dominican Republic. (Although most commonly referred to as CAFTA, the full name of the agreement is the U.S.–Dominican Republic–Central America Free Trade Agreement; it is occasionally referred to as DR–CAFTA because the Dominican Republic was rolled into the treaty following its negotiation in Central America.) My colleague Alejandro Cerón and I found that, despite responding to a uniform text, the process of its implementation was quite varied across member countries (Cerón and Godoy 2009; Godoy and Cerón 2011).

These findings left me both deeply concerned that so little attention was being paid to this issue in the Central American context and troubled that so few Central American health advocates were immersed in these issues. In response to this perceived need, I sought and obtained support from the Ford Foundation to carry out a range of activities on intellectual property and health rights with Central American public health researchers, aiming to build capacity in the region for engagement with this highly technical issue. Jointly with Alejandro Cerón, I spearheaded the creation of a network of public health researchers from across Central America, called the Central American Network on Intellectual Property and Access to Medicines (or Red CEPIAM, by its initials in Spanish) to monitor IP's effects in the context of national and international commitments to the right to health. The participating researchers, who ranked among the region's leading figures in public health policy, conducted studies of IP implementation in their countries and shared their findings with civil society, government, and intragovernmental groups like the Pan-American Health Organization. Discussions with these researchers and our counterparts in Colombia—where network meetings were held—provided me invaluable perspective on how this global issue connected to Central American realities.

In some ways, this intervention was guided by a classic top-down approach to the problem, characteristic of transnational advocacy networks: Thanks to research already conducted elsewhere, and championed by the global access to medicines campaigns led by Doctors Without Borders, Oxfam, and others, we already knew the dangers of intellectual property, but what we lacked was specific data about how those dangers might manifest themselves in particular Central American countries. By involving leading Central American public health researcher-advocates in this data-gathering exercise, we hoped to fill the information void and spur greater attention to this issue in the region as the results of these studies were shared.

Over the course of this work, however, my perspective changed. What I had originally interpreted as a lack of capacity for engaging IP in Central

America turned out to be a commentary on the diversity of possible understandings of health rights and the differences of power and perspective in transnational advocacy networks. The story this book tells, therefore, is primarily the product of a second, related set of explorations of Central American intellectual property issues. Through a series of in-depth interviews conducted over the course of four years, I approached these questions from a more bottom-up approach focusing on the experiences and perspectives of a range of actors in three Central American countries: Costa Rica, El Salvador, and Guatemala.

I selected these particular countries for various reasons. Costa Rica was an obvious choice, given its universal health care system; though all Central American countries embrace—on paper—the idea that health is a human right, only Costa Rica comes close to making the right a reality for most of its people, so it was vitally important to understand how such a successful health system might be affected by new IP norms. Guatemala was also clearly important to include, as the region's largest economy and the site of its most visible tussles over intellectual property policy—and, at one point, the country with the most aggressive data protection policies anywhere in the world. And El Salvador posed other interesting puzzles: Although the country had seen massive mobilization in defense of health rights in the 1990s, on the question of IP and medicines its civil society had been strangely silent; the local generic industry even made public statements expressing tepid support for the trade deal. So I carried out interviews in all three sites, not to test a single hypothesis with three case studies but rather to inform a more open-ended set of questions about the politics behind IP policy and their implications for the transformative potential of human rights.

My interviewees included members of trade agreement negotiating teams, pharmaceutical industry executives, public health advocates, medical practitioners, patients involved in organizations working on access to medicines issues, members of national legislatures, health sector unions, human rights lawyers involved in access cases, judges, officials of state health institutions, and staffers in intellectual property offices. In many cases I held follow-up conversations with the same people in subsequent years and was invited to observe meetings or participate in discussions of related issues.

I found that although many were willing to reiterate the public position they or their allies had already taken in CAFTA debates—most had a sound bite ready on the matter when I first contacted them—when it came to explaining the reasons behind those positions or the political alignments that produced them, many spoke only with considerable caution. Given the inflammatory nature of public accusations lobbed across ideological divides on this issue and my eagerness for people to speak candidly, I took handwritten notes during those conversations rather than recording them, and I agreed not to publish interviewees' names without their permission. Many are cited anonymously in these pages.

I believe this bottom-up perspective is fundamental to understanding the counterhegemonic potential—and indeed the possible pitfalls—of transnational rights campaigns. Yet it is relatively uncommon. As David Engel suggests in a 2012 essay, the dominant way in which scholars approach human rights is by tracing the flow of ideas and practices from the transnational level, where they are presumed to exist in their most potent form, down to the local level, where they may manifest themselves differently due to variations in culture, context, or capacity. Rights, in this formulation, are assumed to be the agent of transformation, though they may become muted or muddled as they encounter obstacles posed by the specific local realities. Engel argues instead for a "horizontal" approach to rights, focusing more broadly on the multiplicity of ways communities conceptualize conflicts and the place (or lack thereof) of rights in localized understandings.

My contribution here is somewhat different, though complementary. In this book, I seek to understand perceptions of rights, politics, and power among differently situated actors—not only among Engel's "ordinary people" but through access to medicines activists, drug company representatives, chronically ill patients, doctors, lawyers, and trade justice advocates. How do each of these people view the struggles over trade agreements, rights, and medicines? Where do they imagine the possibilities for transformative change?

Through these conversations, I learned that Central Americans—from chronically ill patients to human rights lawyers to progressive health advocates—had their own rights visions that didn't quite match up with the discourses offered by transnational access to medicines advocates. While the dominant "vertical" perspective on rights might lead us to explain the variability of discourses as the result of the permutations occasioned when global concepts touch down in different local contexts and are transformed in that encounter, I suggest instead that the Central American visions of rights I detected were equally rooted in global movements and formalized agreements, but often quite different from those espoused by transnational activists. In particular, the understanding of health as a human right offered by Central American progressive health advocates actually represented a more radical and potentially transformative interpretation than the almost quintessentially neoliberal rendering of rights promoted under the banner of access to medicines. There are multiple possible imaginings of rights, and which ones rise to prominence in a given historical moment or geographical setting is more a reflection of politics and power among the actors advocating each approach than it is a reflection of the degree of inherent resemblance to idealized concepts in international agreements. Yet the relationships between these competing ideas, and the transformative possibilities of each, become visible only when one takes a broad and bottom-up view; the more familiar, vertical approach to rights campaigns eclipses this diversity of possible understandings because it traces a single discourse's trajectory through the various layers of legal institutions, thus missing the proverbial "dogs that didn't bark" along the way.

In approaching rights this way, I attempt here to take up the challenge posed by Boaventura de Sousa Santos (2002). Santos argues that human rights can be used in hegemonic ways to reinforce capitalist power and domination and indeed that they tend to have such an effect when we emphasize them as the application of some presumed universal aspirations onto concrete settings. Santos terms this "globalized localism," or globalization from above (2002, 16); its effects reinforce rather than challenge preexisting power structures. On the other hand, Santos insists, this is not predetermined: There are other possible incarnations of rights, rooted in what he describes as multicultural rather than universalist understandings, whereby through dialogues across culture and context more truly counterhegemonic understandings of rights might be advanced. "The central task of emancipatory politics of our time," Santos writes, "consists in transforming the conceptualization and practice of human rights from a globalized localism into a cosmopolitan project" (2002, 18). This book is an attempt to analyze the extent to which the campaigns around intellectual property in Central America accomplished this goal and what broader lessons we might discern from their experience about human rights and the global economy.

Of course, even among Central Americans, a vast diversity of conceptions and practices of rights exist. Part of what makes a given incarnation transformative may stem from the way rights are imagined—the particular pastiche of local and cosmopolitan visions they contain—but part may derive from the way they are deployed: as a rhetorical cry issued to rally activist sentiment, a legal category invoked to constrain others' action, or an argument advanced to legitimate claims before a given authority. The key to understanding rights' transformative power, then, is not linked to capturing something in their inherent essence but rather encountering and assessing them in the various settings in which they are deployed, in courtrooms and customs houses, protests and personal appeals.

As Richard Wilson writes, "The sheer ideological promiscuity and slipperiness of rights talk precludes a definitive classification that human rights are inherently 'dominant' or 'hegemonic' and essential to a US-led neoliberal political-economic project, or that they are a universal charter for the liberation of the weak and dispossessed" (2006, 78). To move beyond such simple binaries, Wilson calls for greater examination of the "social life of human rights."

Relatedly, Mark Goodale calls for scholars of human rights to step outside familiar arguments that rights empower or enervate, offering instead a more nuanced analysis of rights. Goodale terms this a critical intellectual history, a "sustained analytical engagement with the idea of human rights as it emerges within social practices in different cultural and historical contexts" (2006, 27). This book, along those lines, seeks to examine what rights actually "do"—how they are lived and imagined, and put into practice, by differently situated actors—in the concrete context of discussions over health and medicines in Central America. In these pages, I examine rights as they're invoked in discourse, in litigation, in legislation, and in everyday practices; my intention in doing so is not to lump these diverse categories of action into an indistinct whole but rather to take into account the multiple ways rights become real.

Rather than attempting to assess the "impact" or "success" of rights campaigns—using a predetermined understanding of what rights are and aim to accomplish—I offer here a more open-ended inquiry into the ways they are interpreted and engaged by those I spoke with in Central America. Such an approach allows us to assess a different dimension of rights' effectiveness, one that begins from the perspective of those these campaigns are designed to serve. By examining these efforts through a bottom-up approach, grounded in the real life of rights, I aim to gauge the extent to which such discourses offer tools for counterhegemonic change.

An Overview of this Book

As already stated, this book is not intended as an empirical accounting of the agreement's impact on health in the region; I have published work to this effect elsewhere (Cerón and Godoy 2009; Godoy and Cerón 2011). Rather, I intend this book as a reflection on the complex politics of human rights in trade, of transnational coalitions for alternative globalization, and of markets and medicines in our world today. CAFTA itself is no longer in the headlines in the United States; in Central America, IP is no longer an issue around which activists rally. But in these pages I explore what we can learn from this case study, about the writing—and resisting—of the increasingly important, yet seldom examined, rules that govern global integration. In essence, the book is written to answer a single overarching question: How useful are the tools and practices of human rights for challenging injustices that spring from global economic structures? On this terrain, do human rights have truly counterhegemonic potential?

In Chapter 2, I offer a brief primer on pharmaceutical IP, arguing that two core visions of IP and access have shaped the history of policy making on this issue. The dominant approach today, promoted by the software and entertainment industries and the governments of the United States and Europe who largely act at industry's behest on these issues, defines ideas as property and seeks to reward those who invest in their development by limiting access. On the other hand, a growing resistance movement, sometimes operating under the banners of "A2K/access to knowledge" or "open access," argues that the current incentive system can and should be reconfigured to reward innovation without stifling progress. In this chapter, I briefly trace the histories of these developments and explain the basic tools of pharmaceutical IP—patents and test data protection—and how they work, laying some necessary groundwork for the arguments in later chapters.

Beyond this, however, I argue that intellectual property has emerged at the crossroads of contemporary thinking about economics and rights at the global level, making it an ideal site at which to study the counter-hegemonic potential of rights campaigning today. In the human rights world, in the last ten years the titans of the global movement have undertaken a dramatic shift in their own thinking about human rights, broadening the scope of their work to include social and economic rights—like the right to health—on equal footing with the more traditional civil and political rights. If health is truly understood as a fundamental right, as a set of policies promoting economic gain at the expense of human lives, IP could scarcely represent a more frontal threat to the core of the human rights movement. At the same time, if somewhat improbably, intellectual property itself has achieved canonical status within the contemporary U.S. trade regime, making it among the most difficult areas of trade policy to contest. In this sense, too, IP is perhaps the ultimate manifestation of bio-power, a central underlying logic of our times. For both "free" trade advocates and human rights activists, then, the battles over IP cut to the core of their movement's priorities. Though the issue may appear obscure to the uninitiated, it is precisely through the balancing of these contending forces that central tenets in globalization's rule book are being written.

In Chapter 3, I delve into the particularities of intellectual property in the Central American context. After tracing some of the region's principal health problems and describing the basic contours of its health systems, I explain the IP provisions CAFTA requires of its signatory states and show how the national implementation process has sometimes led to even more stringent policies than those required by the agreement. From there, I offer a more detailed discussion of the challenges to measuring the agreement's impact in human rights terms.

These measurement challenges matter greatly because the ability to put clear, convincing information about human rights abuses into the hands of advocates around the globe has always been the currency of the human rights movement. Campaigns rise or fall dependent on their ability to generate outrage in communities halfway around the world; the avail-ability of images and other forms of incontrovertible evidence is key to convincing a global public burdened with compassion fatigue to sign a petition, contact their legislator, attend another rally. How, then, do advo-cates reckon with a slippery, elusive, difficult to prove, and ultimately ob-tuse area like intellectual property? Merely demonstrating the existence of a rights abuse requires complex (and ultimately questionable) econometric calculations; there are no photos of torture victims to shock the public, no epauletted general on whom to heap the blame, not even a ready head count of victims, because the shifting terrain of health decision making makes it impossible to identify specific individuals who will die as a result of IP policy. In light of this, access advocates are left to project future drug prices, arguing that, through a reduction of competition, intellectual prop-erty will prop up artificially high prices and deny access in a broad sense. While studies along these lines can and do predict large impacts on pric-ing, it remains to be seen whether projected prices motivate protests in the same way as the visible suffering of flesh-and-blood victims.

And, perhaps even more important, I argue, these price projections may misjudge the heart of human rights concerns. The very way in which we go about generating the calculations may unwittingly reinscribe certain assumptions about the roles of market and state in providing access. In arguing that low competition drives up prices and therefore limits access, we fail to acknowledge, first of all, that much of what the drug market pro-duces is already unnecessary, and second, that drug markets, especially in small countries like those of Central America, are not particularly compet-itive even without the introduction of IP. In other words, access to medi-cines arguments typically rest on an astonishingly neoliberal claim: the assertion that IP is harmful because it limits market competition, when in fact market competition—particularly in the small markets of Central America—has already shown itself to be an abject failure as an adjudicator of health rights. Is it wise to advocate for failed market mechanisms in the name of human rights? Shouldn't a truly counterhegemonic discourse dig deeper?

In particular, I argue, arguments based on projected pricing alone tend to ignore the pivotal role of the state in health decision making. This is perhaps ironic, given that the human rights movement has long been accused of being overly state-centric and of failing to perceive or challenge the influence of global economic forces on human rights outcomes. In this particular instance, the opposite appears to have occurred; far from focusing excessively on state accountability, the global access to medicines movement targets major drug companies and the Northern Hemisphere governments who do their bidding, while granting the states of Central America something of a free pass.

In Chapter 4, I argue that this is one of many ways in which global access advocates' arguments seemed somewhat out of sync with the vision of Central American health activists. When humanitarian organizations like Oxfam and Doctors Without Borders, trade justice groups like Public Citizen, and to a lesser extent traditional human rights groups like Amnesty International all turned their attention to health in Central America in the context of the CAFTA debates, Central American health activists welcomed the attention to the region's needs. But in interviews some later admitted quietly that they found the emphasis on intellectual property to the exclusion of other problems slightly out of step with their own priorities. This explained, in part, their reluctance to define IP as a central struggle at the time.

Indeed, Central America had been the site of important struggles over health policy long before CAFTA came to town. Most of the battles waged by progressive health advocates in the late twentieth century focused on improving the delivery of state services and tackling the socioeconomic vectors of ill health. Under such a paradigm, questions of access to the latest high-tech medicines—those affected by patents and test data protection—are important, but less so than ensuring access to primary health care for all or promoting improved outcomes through community-based, participatory interventions like the delivery of potable water or improved sanitation systems. Seen this way, intellectual property is a concern, but not a paramount one.

Ultimately, what I (and others aligned with the transnational access to medicines movement) had initially read as a lack of capacity on the part of Central American health activists actually reflected something very different: a commitment to long-standing local struggles, which led to a distinct ordering of priorities. In light of this limited uptake of IP by local health advocates, however, global campaigners often turned to Central

American generic drugmakers to fill the information gap. Although in some countries—Guatemala and Costa Rica—generics producers briefly allied themselves with those organizing against the trade agreement, these alliances were short lived and sat awkwardly with long-standing political alignments.

This disconnect between local and transnational frames in the CAFTA context has important implications for the way we think about human rights. First, far from advancing a uniquely "local" perspective, Central American health leaders traced their ideas to participation in transnational discussions around health like those of the People's Health Movement and grounded their commitments in international agreements like the Declaration of Alma-Ata. In other words, if gaps emerge between the vision of health rights embraced by Central American health advocates and that promoted by transnational groups concerned about IP, these gaps should not be understood as reflective of a transnational discourse having become distorted through its "translation" to the local setting, as a vertical approach to rights consciousness might lead us to believe. Rather, they indicate that multiple ways of understanding health rights were available to Central American advocates, each of them rooted in transnational movements and shaped by particular understandings of where priorities should lie.

Returning to the ideas of Boaventura de Sousa Santos, then, and the core question motivating this book, the key to rights' counterhegemonic potential lies less in the success of the top-down "translation" of a previously articulated norm and more in the emergence of a truly multicultural (to use Santos's 2002 term) conversation around what rights might mean. If we are to gauge the counterhegemonic potential of rights practices in any given struggle, we must examine the specific content of what is being advanced under the banner of rights, for not all rights discourses are equally transformative, and we must evaluate the extent to which it builds on local priorities, rather than simply plugging local realities into an already-formulated global equation for change.

Relatedly, then, we must examine the lived experience of rights, as Wilson (2006) suggests—not only how they are understood by various parties, but the work they "do" when invoked in concrete contexts. Chapter 5 takes up this challenge by looking at the way in which the patients' rights movement has achieved success in Guatemala through litigation for access to medicines, supported through the intervention of the office of the human rights ombudsman. While access litigation has been studied in other national contexts, the Guatemalan case presents a surprising example in many ways, for it is certainly not a context in which one would expect a "rights revolution," yet thousands of patients have obtained access to drugs by invoking human rights mechanisms before the Guatemalan courts.

At the same time, a closer examination of these cases reveals that, in many instances, plaintiffs obtained access to drugs that would not have been allowed them through the normal planning mechanisms of the Guatemalan Social Security Institute—in many cases because the drug in question was deemed not to be cost effective, often because of the availability of a cheaper generic alternative. In other words, in a significant minority of cases, patients who were given generic drugs turned to the courts for access to more expensive IP-protected drugs, and the courts upheld patients' requests in the name of human rights. On the one hand, for scholars critical of IP practices there is an easy rejoinder here: Patients' associations are often known to be in the pocket of pharmaceutical corporations, and human rights mechanisms can be exploited under such logic. Undoubtedly, this sometimes occurs. Yet I argue that, in the context of a state that fails to ensure the safety of its drug supply, these rights claims made by patients are not entirely unreasonable; the state, here, is failing to uphold its basic regulatory function, and patients can scarcely be blamed for using whatever tools are available to gain access to the drugs they believe to be safest. At the same time, I argue, resolving this human rights question by granting individual access to exorbitantly priced drugs—rather than, say, by ensuring the quality of generics across the board—is shortsighted and reveals some of the pitfalls of applying tried-and-true rights tactics like individual litigation against the state in the arena of social and economic rights.

In this context, then, what is the "work" done by human rights? In the more worrisome of the Guatemalan cases, they serve as the vehicle whereby monopoly provisions made available by IP during the patent period live forever—for patients who resist a switch to a generic medication can turn to the courts and have their right to a specific brand drug upheld. Using the individualized lens that litigation favors, such judgments make sense. But, for the long-term planning purposes of state health systems, litigation undermines the pursuit of a coordinated policy for the efficient distribution of limited resources.

This critique of litigation is not new and indeed has been well discussed by a range of law and society scholars including Scheingold (1974), Tushnet (1984), Rosenberg (1991), and McCann (1994). For the purposes of this book, however, what concerns me is the evidence that, cast against the ineffectiveness of a very weak state, human rights claims shore up rather than undermine intellectual property. This takes us back, then, to the central question of this book: Are human rights an antidote to the advance of neoliberal social policy, or are they the very vehicle through which it advances? To what extent are rights truly counterhegemonic when unleashed against economic power?

Chapter 6 returns to this larger question, situating the foregoing discussions within recent transformations of the global political economy to argue that, as rights struggles expand into the terrain of social and economic rights and capital expands beyond borders to an unprecedented degree, the relationship of rights to capital has shifted in significant ways, producing new challenges and contradictions. While the intellectual property debates may initially appear to be a showdown between human rights and "free" trade, closer examination raises important questions about the ways in which some rights approaches to IP may reinforce, rather than challenge, prevailing power structures.

In fact, the key difference between hegemonic and counterhegemonic incarnations of rights is more complex than a vertical perspective on transnational campaigns would allow us to appreciate. Such approaches suggest that rights concepts flow up and down a sort of sliding scale, in which the degree of transformative power packed by any rights campaign is determined by its proximity to conceptions clearest at the international level; "impact," in such a model, is gauged by the degree to which internationally codified abstractions manifest themselves on the ground in any given context. I argue instead that rights notions are multivalent and overlapping, and some are more counterhegemonic in content than others; oftentimes, those that prosper and rise to prominence may be those that least challenge prevailing structures of power, those that seek to tweak rather than radically reimagine systems for distributing scarce resources in society. But there remains the possibility of a broader discussion, a more unsettling campaign, an overturn of established power through the harnessing of transnational solidarity; as we study the way rights work, we need to refine our frameworks beyond the binaries of North/South, transnational/local, free trade/human rights to ensure that we notice these alternate imaginings where they emerge.

Chapter 2

A Primer on Pharmaceutical Intellectual Property

O N MEETING THE OFFICIALS in charge of negotiating intellectual property agreements for the Central American governments, one of the things that most struck me was their youth. By all accounts, CAFTA's chapter 15 was pivotal to the agreement as a whole—as one observer of the negotiations told me, "The Americans told us, 'We're willing to negotiate on labor or the environment, but chapter 15 is take it or leave it'"—and yet those in charge of its negotiation, at least on the Central American side, were noticeably junior to their counterparts in charge of less contentious fields.

In noting this, I don't mean to imply they were inexpert. I found many of them to be quite competent and engaging, and I found myself surprisingly sympathetic to the challenges they'd confronted in seeking to advance national interests in these complex discussions. Costa Rican IP negotiator Federico Valerio, who graciously received me for an interview in the offices of the Ministry of Foreign Trade in 2007, was a good example. He defined Costa Rica's national interest in intellectual property as "defensive": Given that Costa Rica's pharmaceutical companies do not engage in research toward the development of new drugs and given that the Caja relies on access to low-cost generics to meet the health needs of the population, the country stands to lose more than it gains from the augmented intellectual property protections a TRIPS-plus agreement would bring.[1] His central task as IP negotiator was, therefore, to resist—carefully, so as not to imperil the success of the overall agreement to which his government was already committed, but still, when staring down the vastly more powerful U.S. negotiating team across the table, his job was to hold the line. (Not all Central American trade negotiators understood their task in this way, however; Valerio's Salvadoran counterpart, in particular, adopted a markedly different stance.)

For the most part, health activists were deeply critical of the work of Central American governments as they negotiated the terms of CAFTA. The surname of the Salvadoran minister of the economy and head of his country's negotiating team, Miguel Lacayo, provided fodder for bitter jokes (the word *lacayo* means "lackey" in English). In Costa Rica, Valerio bristled at such accusations, recalling meetings of the Pan American Health Organization at which "barbarities" were uttered about the new intellectual property norms Central American governments had accepted. "I told them," he said, "that that they shouldn't say that to us, but instead to the country that's behind all this—the United States."

The challenge, as Valerio saw it, was striking a balance between compliance with international intellectual property rules—a requirement for a country seeking to benefit from foreign trade—and public health. And it was a formidable challenge, given the interests arrayed on both sides. Yet the debate over these issues seemed to generate more heat than light. Access advocates had been successful in portraying the transnational pharmaceutical industry as devils ("*con cachos y cola*," he said—complete with horns and a tail), in contrast to the "saintly" national producers. But in fact, he said, both national and international drug producers were looking out for their own economic interests. To get to the bottom of it, he insisted, one had to go beyond both sides' arguments in search of the broader public good.

I saw this same dilemma play out in each of the countries studied, in slightly different ways. Understanding not only the specific nuts-and-bolts content of CAFTA's intellectual property chapter, but also the heated and acrimonious context in which it was debated, is vital to comprehending the implications of access to medicines struggles for efforts at trade justice or human rights more broadly. In this chapter, I begin with a very brief discussion of how intellectual property works, explaining key concepts of patents and test data protection. From there, I expand into a discussion of why this matters, not only in practical terms for access to medicines but in broader political terms, for understanding the globalized world in which we live. Throughout this book, I argue that the struggles around intellectual property and access provide a unique window through which to analyze two competing frameworks for organizing global relations: free trade and human rights. In the remainder of this chapter, I discuss the history of these two approaches and their perhaps surprising convergence on this particular corner of administrative law. This sets up not only the context for the particular contestations in Central America discussed in Chapters 3 through 5 but also my attempt to discern broader theoretical lessons from this experience in Chapter 6.

Patents and Test Data: Key Concepts in Pharmaceutical Intellectual Property

Patents are the most widely known form of intellectual property in pharmaceuticals. In the timeline of drug development, a patent is typically sought early in the research process to prevent a competitor from introducing a substantially similar product. Once granted, the patent provides exclusive access to the market for a period beginning at the date when the patent request was first filed. But the drug does not hit the market immediately; after the drug discovery and preclinical phases conclude, clinical trials require several phases of additional testing to demonstrate its safety and efficacy in humans before marketing approval is granted by the health regulatory agency—the U.S. Food and Drug Administration (FDA) or its foreign equivalent—allowing its sale on the market. Thus, pharmaceutical companies have an incentive to complete clinical trials and bring the drug to market as quickly as possible because the clock on their monopoly is ticking. Therefore, although the current patent term is twenty years under U.S. law, Grabowski and Kyle found that between 1995 and 2005 the average *effective* length of pharmaceutical patents in the United States— meaning the period of time that the drug was on the market and granted a monopoly—was 13.5 years (Grabowski and Kyle 2007, 491–502).

Once the patent expires, generic versions of the same drug can immediately enter the market. Generics are typically much cheaper than patented drugs, in part because the regulatory authorities require generics to demonstrate only that they are equivalent to an existing drug already shown to be safe, rather than repeating the lengthy and expensive clinical trials process. When multiple generics enter the market following patent expiry, the competition among them typically fuels a precipitous price drop. Where only a single generic enters, or where generic companies choose to invest heavily in branding strategies, the price reductions are less dramatic (Frank and Salkever 1997).

In addition to bringing their drug to market as quickly as possible so as to maximize the benefits of their patent-granted monopoly, originator drug companies also frequently seek to extend their patents beyond the twenty-year period. They do this either by arguing that they should be granted an extension to compensate for procedural delays in the granting of marketing approval or by introducing slight alterations to the product—changing the color or shape of the pill, for example—and requesting a new patent, a process critics call "evergreening." The WTO's TRIPS Agreement does not establish any international standard as to how countries should deal with these sorts of requests.

Patents, however, are not necessarily the most important form of pharmaceutical intellectual property in all jurisdictions. TRIPS also includes the figure of test data protection, which differs from patents in important ways. While test data protection is in force, generic drugmakers are not allowed to register their drugs by demonstrating only equivalency to a product already shown to be safe, in this sense proving the safety of their drug by "piggybacking" on the clinical test data produced by the originator company. What's protected, in this sense, is the test data. Although theoretically a generic company could enter the market if able to produce its own clinical test data, in practice it would be prohibitively expensive for generic manufacturers to replicate clinical trials, so test data protection, like a patent, produces a temporary monopoly.

What makes test data protection so significant, however, is the fact that, unlike a patent, it is granted *automatically* to the first registrant of any drug at the time of market entry. Patents, on the other hand, require significant investment on the part of the patent seeker; they are granted by national, not international, authorities, so patents must be sought separately before the authorities in each country, and procedures and standards vary from country to country. Typically, patent law requires demonstration that the substance is new, nonobvious, and useful; patents can be challenged by third parties and can be revoked if it is shown that the product does not fulfill these criteria. And many of the new drugs may indeed fail to clear the threshold: For all the discussion about market-driven "innovation," much of what originator pharmaceutical companies have produced in recent years is not particularly innovative, at least in therapeutic terms. In 2003, the U.S. FDA concluded that, although the pharmaceutical industry had been seeking the approval of a greater number of drugs in recent years, a decreasing percentage of that pool represented truly innovative products in therapeutic terms (U.S. Food and Drug Administration 2003). Similarly, a GAO review of FDA data from 1993 to 2005 found that 68 percent of new drug applications were classified by the FDA as modifications of existing drugs (U.S. Government Accountability Office 2006). Furthermore, under certain circumstances patents can be effectively circumvented through the government issuance of a compulsory license in response to a public health emergency.

Granted the cost of securing patent protection in each country, patents' vulnerability to challenges, and the relatively tiny markets that may exist for expensive drugs in poor countries, many originator companies simply don't bother to patent everywhere. This is why Attaran and Gillespie-White's (Attaran and Gillespie-White 2001, 1886–1892) finding that antiretrovirals haven't even been patented in many of the poorest countries of Africa is ultimately unsurprising. This finding doesn't mean patents aren't a problem in more profitable markets, in ways that might have an impact on access in poor countries; for example, given the Indian generic pharmaceutical industry's pioneering role as the "pharmacy to the Third World," the post-2005 tightening of patent law in India has been shown to decrease access in other countries who lack domestic manufacturing capacity and had previously relied on Indian exports to meet local health needs (Doctors Without Borders 2012). Nor does Attaran and Gillespie-White's finding mean that other forms of intellectual property, like test data protection, aren't limiting access in poor countries. For originator companies, the automatic granting of test data protection is a silver bullet: It's applied across the board to all new products whether innovative or not, requires no action on the part of the company, is apparently uncontestable, and keeps competitors off the market.

TRIPS mentions test data protection but does not specify how long the protection should last, so a country can be TRIPS compliant without enacting such mechanisms. Yet as I explain in the following discussion, for advocates of what Sell has called the "maximalist" IP agenda, TRIPS doesn't so much set the standard as provide a floor on which the standard can be built through continual upward pressure (Sell 2010). While powerful global South countries like Brazil have been able to resist incorporating test data protection into their legislation, and savvy midsize nations like Argentina have written their test data legislation in a way that favors access, the countries of the CAFTA region were less able to resist such pressures; as a result, today, test data protection probably poses a more formidable challenge to access in Central America than patents. It is vitally important, then, to resist the tendency to conflate IP with patents because, particularly in the weakest countries where access is often poorest, patents are not the only problem.

How Did We Get Here? Intellectual Property, Human Rights, and Their Rise to Prominence in Global Trade Talks

Peter Drahos divides the history of intellectual property policy making into three phases: territorial, international, and global (Drahos 1997, 201–211). During the *territorial* period, he explains, each nation established its own IP policies, and any protections afforded to innovators ended at the border of the nation-state. In most of the world, medicines were excluded from patentability due to concerns about the public health impact of patent-induced monopolies, and such a decision was understood as falling squarely within the purview of the sovereign state. But this skepticism about the applicability of IP was not limited to medicines: As Boyle argues, thinkers such as Jefferson expressed concerns that the application of copyright to written works would run counter to the public interest in disseminating culture and education (Boyle 2008). From the earliest days of drafting IP law, then, concerns were raised about how to balance private rights with the public good.

As international commerce accelerated in the 1800s, however, European nations began to complain about piracy (mostly of published books) in neighboring countries, leading to bilateral and eventually multilateral agreements to protect copyright holders in one nation against infringement in other member nations. So as history moved into what Drahos terms the *international period*, agreements such as the Paris Convention for the Protection of Industrial Property (1883) and the Berne Convention (1888) for copyright established such principles as nondiscrimination and national treatment, by which member states were obligated to extend the same privileges to citizens of other member states as granted to their own. For Drahos, this approach defines the international period in IP lawmaking, in which sovereign states hammered out agreements to defend their national interests, without attempting to define a single overarching standard.

Significantly, these treaties did not obligate substantive changes in individual nations' laws; IP policy was still determined nationally, and many states continued to exclude pharmaceutical products from patentability well into the twentieth century. This was true even in highly industrialized nations—Germany, for example, first allowed pharmaceutical patents in 1968, Japan in 1976, Switzerland in 1977, and Spain in 1992 (Hestermeyer 2007). What's more, during this period free trade arguments were frequently invoked to criticize IP, resulting even in the abolition of patents in the Netherlands in 1869 (Boyle 2008). Ideas like patent pools and prizes for innovation were embraced as alternative ways to reward innovation. So, although the greater recognition of a need to coordinate certain legal regimes across nations led to new international agreements, core ideas of intellectual property still occupied a tenuous position among free trade advocates suspicious of its monopoly mechanisms.

Yet, in the wake of World War II, major changes were set in motion that would lead, eventually, to a fundamental reordering of the world's political economy. While still reeling from the horrors of the Holocaust, prevailing Western powers convened a series of meetings to discuss new ways of organizing international relations to avoid the disastrous outcomes the world had just seen. One of these meetings, at Bretton Woods, gave birth to the World Bank and International Monetary Fund (IMF) and a set of agreements aimed at organizing countries' participation in the market to avoid the anarchy and insecurity produced when individual nation-states designed monetary policies in incoherent fashion. (Another meeting, at San Francisco, produced the Universal Declaration of Human Rights, which I will discuss shortly—an attempt to promote greater security by placing checks on states' abilities to trample the rights of their citizens.)

Both of these efforts sought solutions in the Enlightenment ideals of individual freedom, but recognized, in a historic step, the need to craft international—not yet transnational—tools to compensate for the failure of individual nation-states. These tools included, as first steps, the agreement on basic rules and the establishment of new multilateral institutions through which nations could work together in pursuit of a stable and prosperous global order.

The agreements achieved at Bretton Woods were historic, representing the first ever agreement among states to regulate the international economy to stimulate and streamline international commerce. The guiding vision behind this international regulation was the notion of free trade, advocated strenuously by the U.S. delegation. Rather than a naked project of U.S. domination or an unabashed defense of economic growth for its own sake, however, the talks at Bretton Woods were described as an exercise in multilateral cooperation for the common good. As the head of the U.S. delegation to the 1944 meetings at Bretton Woods, Treasury Secretary Henry Morgenthau, explained,

> We have to recognize that the wisest and most effective way to protect our national interests is through international cooperation—that is to say, through united effort for the attainment of common goals. This has been the great lesson taught by the war, and is, I think, the great lesson of contemporary life—that the people of the earth are inseparably linked to one another by a deep, underlying community of purpose. . . . To seek the achievement of our aims separately through the planless, senseless rivalry that divided us in the past, or through the outright economic aggression which turned neighbors into enemies would be to invite ruin again upon us all. Worse, it would be once more to start our steps irretraceably down the steep, disastrous road to war. That sort of extreme nationalism belongs to an era that is dead. Today the only enlightened form of national self-interest lies in international accord. At Bretton Woods we have taken practical steps toward putting this lesson into practice in monetary and economic fields. I take it as an axiom that this war is ended; no people—therefore no government of the people—will again tolerate prolonged or wide-spread unemployment. A revival of international trade is indispensable if full employment is to be achieved in a peaceful world and with

standards of living which will permit the realization of man's reasonable hopes." (U.S. Army Information School, Carlisle Barracks, Pa. 1946)

The agreements established a system of capital controls, designed to regulate the world economy such that international trade could proceed without running afoul of sudden currency fluctuations due to rapid depreciations or unreliable exchange rates. The goal was to establish shared rules to ensure predictability and hence profitability for global capitalism.

Yet the growth of multinational corporations in the ensuing decades created problems for this system. Seeking to avoid the controls placed by central banks, corporations invested their money overseas. The growing internationalization of capital created opportunities for speculation and attendant instability, to which the Bretton Woods system, rooted in nation-state regulation, offered no response; growing tensions between the United States, Europe, and Japan led to increasing chafing at the strictures the system imposed. Eventually, the U.S. abandonment of the gold standard in 1971 dealt the system its fatal blow, ushering in a period of currency flexibility.

As William Robinson writes, "The collapse of the Bretton Woods system of fixed currency exchange and national economic regulation via currency controls was the first step in the liberation of embryonic transnational capital from the institutional constraints of the nation-state system. It signaled the beginning of the globalization epoch" (2004:111). The Keynesian system of state regulation was definitively dead.

In addition to establishing set rules governing currency and exchange, however, the talks at Bretton Woods also established key international institutions that endure to this day, among them the International Monetary Fund and the precursor to the World Bank. It was through these institutions that the Washington Consensus was later to emerge, replacing the accords at Bretton Woods with a new set of rules designed specifically to address the economic crises that wracked Latin America in the 1980s. The initial postwar talks also laid the groundwork for the General Agreement on Tariffs and Trade (GATT), originally intended as a short-term alternative during the construction of an enduring International Trade Organization (ITO) dedicated to reducing trade barriers between nations. While the ITO failed, GATT provided the framework for a series of "rounds" or talks, at which participating countries agreed to reduce tariffs to promote free trade. Each round incorporated a progressively larger set of tariff reduction agreements. Eventually, the Uruguay Round from 1986 to 1993 led to the creation of the World Trade Organization, for the first time a supranational entity with adjudicatory and enforcement powers all its own, not rooted in any single state.

As regards IP policy making, the WTO's TRIPS Agreement, which took effect on January 1, 1995, marks the watershed moment for what Drahos calls the *global phase*: For the first time in history, TRIPS established a single standard of minimum IP protections across the globe. The agreement extends both the subject matter to be covered by IP in all WTO member nations (to include not only pharmaceuticals but also chemicals, pesticides, and plant varieties), as well as the term of protection, establishing for the first time a universal twenty-year patent term. And it mandates that all countries alter their domestic legislation to include these standards or face sanctions in a WTO tribunal.

Yet although the steady progression to uniform global trade standards enshrined in the WTO responded to broad geopolitical trends—in other words, this development is not unique to IP, by any stretch of the imagination—IP's inclusion as a central tenet of what is today taken as "free" trade was anything but a foregone conclusion. For the first fifty years following Bretton Woods, countries were free to design and enforce their own IP policies. The U.S. government did not begin to link trade and intellectual property rights enforcement until the 1980s (Sell and Prakash 2004, 156). As Sell and Prakash argue, establishing international standards for the protection of intellectual property rights was not a major component of discussions of economic liberalization until the successful campaign waged by the pharmaceutical industry in the 1980s and 1990s, in which "the business network grafted its agenda [of IP protection] onto the established American norm of free trade and the government's attendant preoccupation with competitiveness" (Sell and Prakash 2004, 158).

And not only was this regime's eventual emergence not inevitable, in many ways its specific tenets represent a paradox. As Sell (2003) explains, the primary aims of U.S. trade negotiators in the Uruguay Round of GATT talks were extending the dominant trend of deregulation and trade liberalization, yet in IP they were asked to impose new restrictions on open competition, to effectively erect barriers to market access. Indeed, this contradiction has forced some promoters of archetypal "free" trade policies into increasingly contorted positions.

For example, in a 2005 study, Homedes and her colleagues ask why, after their own economists recommended health policy reforms to bring down pharmaceutical prices through increased competition, the World Bank's policy reforms did nothing to challenge the anticompetitive practices of IP in Latin America (Homedes, Ugalde, and Rovira Forns 2005, 691). The Bank's 1993 World Development Report recommends the use of essential drug lists to concentrate purchases and bring down prices, the use of generics to avoid monopoly pricing, and the adoption of stronger mechanisms to control the industry's use of anticompetitive marketing tactics. All of these efforts would be hamstrung by heightened IP. Yet subsequent World Bank assistance packages allocated funds to the purchase of drugs without implementing any of these policies. Ultimately, the authors suggest that the Bank effectively abandoned its own suggestions because of the "neoliberal ideology of World Bank decision-makers"—reinforced through such things as a Pharmaceutical Manufacturers Association of America (PhRMA) sponsored fellowship at the Bank headquarters and the outsize influence of the U.S. government as a dominant voice in Bank policy (Homedes, Ugalde, and Rovira Forns 2005, 709). Asking why the World Bank has been so strangely silent as debates heated up around intellectual property and access to medicines, despite being on record as supporting the aforementioned policies, they conclude, "It would have been difficult for the agency to take a position against its principal shareholders" (Homedes, Ugalde, and Rovira Forns 2005, 710).

The deep irony of intellectual property policy today is that, in the name of "free" trade, governments have embraced policies that artificially restrict competition by forestalling market access and propping up monopoly prices—precisely the opposite of what "free" trade is usually taken to mean. For this reason, when referring to contemporary trade agreements that include anticompetitive intellectual property provisions, I believe it is more accurate to avoid the "free" trade moniker entirely or to place the term within quotation marks as an acknowledgment of its hypocrisy. Similarly, this calls into question the frequent invocation—by critics—of the term *neoliberal*: If it's "neoliberal" ideology that prevents the adoption of reforms grounding social policy in more efficient and competitive market mechanisms, what does *neoliberal* even mean? The terms have become meaningless. Although IP is not the only site of contradiction in contemporary U.S. trade policy, it is the element that most obviously gives the lie to the elaborate fiction that "neoliberal" "free trade" policies are based on any coherent set of principles, values, or ways of understanding our world, rather than the naked defense of powerful economic interests.

Over time, then, the discourse and practices of trade liberalization have experienced some significant shifts. First, the agreements, and the venues for their enforcement, have shifted from the interstate to suprastate levels. Today, states undeniably continue to play a key role in trade debates, but these discussions are increasingly subordinated to global market logic. And second, while the spread of "free" trade is often imagined as a geographic process—the law's steady blanketing of ever larger sections on a map—in fact its spread has been as much topical as it has been spatial. The issues considered germane to trade discussions have mushroomed, with contemporary agreements penetrating into state welfare policy, including areas such as education and health care once considered the exclusive purview of domestic policy. Nowhere is this more clearly illustrated than in the rising tide of intellectual property law and its application. Intellectual property law, which permits the patenting of life itself such that its economic benefits can be delivered coherently through market relations, is the example par excellence of the dominance of the market as the central logic for organizing social life.

The field of intellectual property law today is extraordinarily lucrative, and its practitioners are politically powerful, for IP has come to serve as the lynchpin of U.S. corporate hegemony in the twenty-first-century "knowledge economy." As Wayne Paugh, acting U.S. coordinator for international intellectual property enforcement, stated on World Intellectual Property Day 2008, "From the United States' perspective, intellectual property represents $5.5 trillion, which is almost half of our entire GDP" (Paugh 2008). IP law, in this context, is the set of rules that corporate leaders in this new economy have advocated to preserve their position.

After all, the rules laid down to govern trade in previous generations protected U.S. interests through things like tariffs and trade preferences, but as the industrial economy waned in the late twentieth century, new challenges arose. For the most part, what U.S. corporations "sell" today is ideas; yet protecting the profits reaped from the use of these intangible assets is ever harder as the products they generate traverse borders with unprecedented ease. Thanks to new technologies, many of the results of these ideas are readily replicable at low cost. How, then, do Big Pharma, Microsoft, the entertainment industry, and other titans of postindustrial capitalism hold on to their advantage? It is precisely this anxiety that drives growing interest in rewriting the rules that govern patents and trademarks in increasingly far-flung nations. As a U.S. consular official in China recently told a reporter from the *New York Times*, "Nothing has a higher priority in our trade policy than the fight to protect American intellectual property. It is every bit as important an effort for us as the war against weapons of mass destruction" (Fishman 2005).

The Human Rights Paradigm

Yet "free" trade is not the only metanarrative through which to understand the ordering of economic and political relationships in our contemporary world. Indeed, just as the spirit of Bretton Woods sought to liberalize economic relations as a way to create order and stability in the global economic order, a related spirit emerged in San Francisco during the talks that gave rise to the Universal Declaration of Human Rights in 1948. The rights regime, like the "free" trade paradigm, has undergone several transformations over the decades, as shown in Table 2.1.

At the time of their conception, economic and political liberalization were assumed to be compatible, mutually reinforcing developmental logics; economies "opened" to global forces were assumed to produce more politically free peoples and vice versa.[2] The contemporary human rights discourse, though it has roots in eighteenth-century Enlightenment ideals, also experienced a defining moment at the end of the 1940s, with the adoption of the Universal Declaration of Human Rights (UDHR) by the UN General Assembly in 1948. The document itself contemplates a holistic vision of rights, placing social and economic rights on equal footing with civil and political rights; as Mary Ann Glendon (2001) shows, this was largely at the urging of Southern Hemisphere actors. Yet it was not to last.

Almost immediately after its passage, political pressure in the United States and Western Europe focused on the civil and political rights in the

TABLE 2.1 Trade Liberalization and the Developing Rights Regime

	Post-WW2	Cold War	Post-Cold War
"Free" trade	• Interstate agreements to regulate international commerce and fiscal policy (Bretton Woods) • Trade discussions limited in scope • Active role for state in managing economy	• GATT expands to cover a wider range of economic sectors, reducing tariffs to promote free trade • Fissures appear and grow in the system of currency controls • Eventual collapse of Bretton Woods agreements	• Supranational institutions (WTO) and transnational trade agreements • Much more expansive scope for trade talks • Unfettered capitalism
	↕ COMPATIBLE ↕	↕ COMPATIBLE ↕	↕ COMPETING ↕
Human rights	• Interstate agreements • Full panoply of rights	• Limited focus on civil/political rights	• Supranational institutions (ICC) and transnational enforcement of domestic human rights laws • Expansion to social/economic rights

declaration, at the strict exclusion of social and economic rights. The succeeding covenants to implement the UDHR into law crystallize the separation in unambiguous terms: As Douzinas explains,

> The civil and political rights covenant creates a state duty "to respect and ensure to all" the listed rights. The economic and social rights treaty is much more flexible and equivocal: member states undertake "to take steps, individually and through international assistance and cooperation . . . with a view to achieving progressively the full realization" of the covenant rights. (Douzinas 2007)

In T. H. Marshall's classic formulation, securing civil and political rights lay at the core of the human rights struggle, while social, economic, and cultural rights were relegated to secondary and tertiary tiers. Amnesty International, similarly, was founded on the presumption that civil and political rights—the denial of which was epitomized in the archetypal figure of the prisoner of conscience—were the foundation for the enjoyment of other rights and thus afforded a higher priority for action. The United Nations, too, built its human rights work on the concept of "generations of rights," in which civil and political rights were granted primary importance.

Once assured by this defining down (if not outright dismissal) of social and economic rights, some U.S. Cold Warriors came to regard human rights as a powerful discourse in their ideological battles against communism. In this framework, as Dezalay and Garth (2006) show, institutions like the International Commission of Jurists emerged as early leaders in the human rights field, though their approach was inextricably bound to the process of defending and promoting U.S. capitalist hegemony, and their reading of which rights mattered was undeniably shaped by that project (Dezalay and Garth 2006). The first major test of the emergent human rights paradigm was not posed by the Soviet Union, however, but by Latin America, where authoritarian regimes (this time mostly of the right) engaged in the systematic use of torture, "disappearances," and extrajudicial executions against the opposition (this time mostly on the left). Even staunch anticommunists like those at the Ford Foundation recognized the similarities between Pinochet's tactics and those of the Soviets and became involved as supporters of human rights. Gradually, the field staked out some autonomy from the U.S. foreign policies that supported the dictators (Dezalay and Garth 2006). The now-familiar insistence on human rights as an impartial set of commitments that transcend politics is a result of that bid for independence.

Given the provenance of such ideas and especially their historic ties to U.S. imperialism, many Latin American leftists, particularly those who were actively engaged in trying to promote socialism, did not initially voice their concerns in the language of rights—or at least not in *this* language of rights. Latin America has a distinctive rights tradition, as discussed in Chapter 3; although often assumed to be derivative of U.S. and European traditions, in fact Latin American constitutions reveal an approach to rights less libertarian and more grounded in social and economic rights than the dominant narrative of human rights more familiar in the North (Wright-Carozza 2003; Glendon 2003). In any case, faced with the systematic brutality of state terrorism, and noting that framing claims in the liberal language of individual rights conferred access to a broader audience of potential allies, many Latin American reformers began to articulate human rights claims, thus engaging in a new sort of North–South transaction. As Dezalay and Garth explain,

> Just as the Chilean opposition had been able to gain some power and credibility within Chile through this connection to a discourse of human rights coming largely from the north, those in the north who were questioning the traditional Cold War strategies could build their own positions by investing in the same discourse and the struggles in Chile and elsewhere. (2006, 241)

Organizations like Amnesty obtained the campaign materials needed to legitimate their efforts while (some) Southern dissidents secured their survival. The early campaigns on Chile were thus very successful and wound up shaping the tactics of the human rights movement for decades to come. In fact, one might argue that it was the Southern Cone experience that effectively launched human rights as a true movement with broad-based civil society participation, not merely a discourse of lawyers and legislators.

In the wake of the Cold War, the discourse has enjoyed unprecedented success; Costas Douzinas calls human rights "the credo of the new world order," dating its triumph to 1989 (Douzinas 2007). Yet the transition to this new world order has also brought with it some reform of core principles. Leading forces in the human rights movement undertook significant processes of rethinking in the late 1990s and the early twenty-first century. These changes, detailed in the following discussion, bring human rights to an important crossroads today—a point at which the treatment of intellectual property provides an important test case, the success or failure of which will have important implications for future directions.

Beginning in the 1990s, major Northern Hemisphere human rights organizations began to reconsider their historic hierarchy of rights. The Balkans crisis posed an important challenge to the movement, as a chorus of feminist critics charged that human rights groups downplayed the systematic use of sexual violence as a weapon of war. In focusing on state violence, critics like Catharine MacKinnon and Susan Brownmiller charged, human rights tended to perceive that violence that affected women was "private," the result of individual passions gone awry or crimes of opportunity run amok in the context of wartime lawlessness, rather than state policy. The critique was extended to domestic violence outside the wartime context; human rights groups had long reacted with paralysis to crimes against women because it could not be proven that the *state* was systematically behind the abuse. As such critiques gained momentum, it became clear that human rights groups had to hold states accountable for *in*action in the case of violence against women. By the end of the 1990s, a number of high-visibility campaigns surrounding the killings of women in Ciudad Juárez and Chihuahua, Mexico—and later in Guatemala—revealed significant attempts by mainstream human rights groups like Amnesty International to rectify this problem. Today, more and more human rights campaigns focus on states as failing to protect rights when they are assailed by private forces. This is an important change[3] from past practice and an attempt to transcend the limitations of state-centrism.

At the same time, a related set of challenges emerged that questioned not only the targets but also the scope of human rights action. As struggles over issues loosely termed "globalization"—ranging from the Narmada Dam project in India to oil exploitation in the Niger Delta to the privatization of water in Bolivia—made clear, the center of gravity in global justice was shifting. In many countries, especially in the Americas, the principal threat no longer seemed to be brutally repressive dictatorships but ineffectual, corrupt, or inept regimes that allowed corporations to run roughshod over the rights of local populations.

The more Northern leaders of the human rights world heard about these struggles over resource exploitation and sweatshops and access to affordable medications, the clearer it became that, if human rights were to remain relevant in the twenty-first century, they had to make sense in the Global South where freedom of thought and expression, of organization and affiliation, were held hostage not by military dictatorships but by hunger, poverty, and disease. Indeed, the state of affairs in Latin America at the dawn of the twenty-first century presented the ultimate indictment of the old model T. H. Marshall had proposed, where the securing of civil and political rights would naturally enable the subsequent securing of social and economic rights: Dictatorships had been defeated, but hunger ran free.

Moreover, the chance to focus on rights in a broader context also enabled the human rights movement to respond to critics who charged that its leaders fancied themselves saviors. As Douzinas charges, "Humanitarian campaigns in the West . . . place the Westerner in the role of a savior who rescues Third World victims from their evil compatriots" (Douzinas 2007). Kennedy similarly criticizes human rights' politics of representation, arguing that "the remove between human rights professionals and the people they purport to represent can reinforce a global divide of wealth, mobility, information, and access to audience. Human rights professionals consequently struggle . . . against a tide of bad faith, orientalism, and self-serving sentimentalism" (Kennedy 2004). During the Cold War, as Dezalay and Garth argue, the invocation of Chilean human rights violations gave Amnesty and other groups legitimacy as they sought to carve out space for international human rights. Yet, with the decline of dictatorships and growing awareness of the role of the global economy and its legal and political apparati as frequent sources, not solutions, to human rights problems, the representation question arose again. To generate legitimate and relevant cases, human rights groups of the North had to address Southern problems and incorporate such perspectives or face charges of neoimperialism.

Throughout the 1990s and into the 2000s, Amnesty International expanded its mandate to include an ever-wider set of abuses and constituencies. In 2001, at the biennial meeting of the organization's highest decision-making body, delegates approved a historic plan to work on all forms of abuses, including denials of social and economic rights, for the first time in the organization's history. In 2003, the same body adopted a resolution to reframe the organization's work in ways that would tackle issues like rights to food and water. This move to integrate rights was not unique to Amnesty; the United Nations also abandoned the terminology "generations of rights," focusing instead on their interdependence, and other organizations like Human Rights Watch began to engage social and economic rights around the same time.

And, in a related set of developments, human rights burst its britches. The discourse outgrew the organizations that had worked to establish its legitimacy and began to serve as the banner for a range of humanitarian and development organizations like Oxfam, Doctors Without Borders, and others. Today, the right to development has become a central discourse in antipoverty efforts. The right to health, too, has gained prominence within progressive public health circles as a new way to frame the old struggle for social medicine. If anything, the diversification of work undertaken by organizations like Amnesty follows, rather than leads, this explosion of "rights talk" in virtually all spheres of social justice and humanitarian work.

As regards health, the field of "health and human rights" has given a new name to long-standing struggles for health equity. Initially a product of activist efforts to demand state responses to the HIV/AIDS crisis, the discursive success of the health and human rights approach has infused old struggles for social medicine with new optimism and embedded them within new institutional frameworks (Gruskin and Tarantola 2002). In many ways, this newly minted generation of health and human rights experts has taken up the tools of rights in novel ways; for example, they now lead the field in engaging intellectual property debates. Today, the cutting-edge human rights arguments against hegemonic interpretations of IP are offered by Oxfam, Doctors Without Borders, and others, though Amnesty, Human Rights Watch, and even some committees of the UN system have also issued statements endorsing counterhegemonic visions. In Oxfam's Make Trade Fair, or Doctors Without Borders' Campaign on Essential Medicines, we see human rights approaches invoked on an issue that, decades ago, would have been framed in very different terms, considered to fall outside the scope of what human rights was all about. And in important ways, these campaigns seek to target new culprits; no longer state centric, they take on the global system, including trade rules, corporate policies, and state practices.

So human rights, like free trade, has gone global, both in its geographic aspirations and in its empirical focus. A set of tools originally elaborated to hold nation-states accountable, it is now being stretched in new directions as the movement's historic lessons become just one set in a growing global search for tools to tackle the abuses of capital. As of yet, no clear direction has emerged in this amorphous global justice movement, which includes human rights groups and efforts but transcends them. Boycotts, street protests at trade talks, fair trade and buy local campaigns, and the Occupy or Los Indignados movements are among the tactics being explored to further this broader set of human rights objectives. There is no clear leader nor co-ordinating body, no strategic direction mapped out; but, as Boaventura de Sousa Santos (2005) argues, perhaps the insistence on plural possibilities is the genius of today's diffuse efforts at counterhegemonic cosmopolitanism. Writing about the World Social Forum, he argues,

> As the first critical utopia of the twenty-first century, the WSF aims to break with the tradition of the critical utopias of Western modernity, many of which turned into conservative utopias. The openness of the utopian dimension of the WSF is rooted in its attempt to escape this perversion. For the WSF, the claim of alternatives is plural." (Santos 2005, 47)

But like any moment imbued with great promise, there are also formidable perils in the path of human rights. And it is here that I return to the importance of intellectual property and the central concerns of this book: When "free" trade advocates and human rights advocates both claim the authority to dictate policy on this contentious issue—as, indeed, they do today—which side wins, and what are the implications of that victory? In the following section, I first describe the heated debates held between the proponents of these dueling paradigms, and then some of the real-world clashes that have unfolded in recent years around this issue.

Clashes between Free Trade and Human Rights on Intellectual Property

Proponents of today's stricter intellectual property system, of course, argue that it harnesses the market for the benefit of all: Short-term monopolies provide profit incentives to reward those who discover new drugs, propelling scientific research into as-yet-undiscovered cures for deadly diseases. Pharmaceutical companies are private corporations that invest millions in the high-risk gamble of developing new drugs; without a mechanism to ensure that they recoup their investment, there would be no incentive for them to innovate and hence very little hope that new therapies could be developed for deadly diseases. Under this conception, patents and other intellectual property protections *increase*, rather than limit, access to medicines because they create incentives for innovation in the first place and because, when patents expire, generics can introduce low-cost copies of the previously protected drugs, thus ensuring their broad availability (Herrling 2007, 174–175).

At the same time, however, a broad and diverse movement has emerged to contest this hegemonic approach to intellectual property. There are those who see the transformations made possible by new technologies as potential engines for development in previously excluded areas of the globe, embracing Thomas Friedman's idea that "the world is flat"—or can be, if the rules governing globalization prioritize open access. A broad coalition of groups, sometimes referred to as the Access to Knowledge, or A2K, movement, see the urgent push to enhance IP protection as threatening to foreclose such possibilities. Their concerns are not limited to medicines. Critics of the new IP regime have also objected to the impact on small-scale agricultors of patented, genetically modified seeds, which require purchase at every planting season. Others decry the fact that plants and substances used for centuries by indigenous peoples can now be owned and controlled by Northern corporations. Some denounce the implications of patented human gene sequences or diagnostic techniques on bioethical grounds, arguing that private ownership of such assets inherently limits scientific discovery. Similarly, advocates of open source software raise alarms about the way the use of proprietary information technology forestalls the free circulation of ideas. And others, including those featured in this book, warn that the application of intellectual property to pharmaceutical products limits the availability of affordable medicines, condemning poor patients to go without; as economist Joseph Stiglitz puts it, the debates over IP and medicines pit "life versus profits" (Stiglitz 2006).

For Stiglitz and organizations like Doctors Without Borders, Oxfam, Knowledge Ecology International, and Health GAP, IP impedes access because it rewards innovation through the granting of market monopolies. This system encourages investment in only those diseases that afflict those who can afford to pay for drugs and does so through mechanisms that keep prices higher than they would be in a competitive market. For patients in poor countries, then, this creates a tragic double jeopardy: When they fall ill to diseases that disproportionately affect the world's poor, like Chagas, no new drugs are available because there has been insufficient incentive for investment, and when they fall ill with diseases that also afflict the wealthy, like cancer or hypertension, the new drugs are priced out of their reach. Though critics disagree on whether prizes for innovation, patent pools, or other approaches represent the best alternative to the current system, they agree that society can and should ensure that those who develop drugs for deadly diseases reap a financial reward without balancing the system on the backs of the poor.

And they have scored some impressive victories, despite the hegemonic power of pro-IP forces. In the wake of TRIPS, successful transnational activism pulled the pendulum back toward access in subsequent years. Two landmark victories from this period reflect activists' growing ability to generate public outrage over intellectual property and capitalize on it for policy change. The first occurred when, in response to massive organizing by civil society in South Africa and the United States, the U.S. government agreed in 2000 to drop a case it had sought to bring against the government of South Africa at the WTO. In that case, the United States had argued that, in instituting policies that took advantage of TRIPS's limited flexibilities to import generic versions of patented HIV medications, South Africa was violating its obligations under international law. A vibrant coalition of vocal and highly visible AIDS organizations argued, in turn, that in the face of the epidemic ravaging the African continent, denying South Africans the ability to access affordable drugs was tantamount to slaughter. Aggressive transnational campaigning tactics by ACT UP (AIDS Coalition to Unleash Power) and other AIDS activists were particularly successful in targeting then presidential candidate Al Gore for his role in sanctioning South Africa. Ultimately, the activists won in the court of public opinion, and the legal case was abandoned before the WTO tribunal could rule on the matter.

A second victory came at the WTO itself when, after years of coalition-building work by numerous Global South countries, the issue of IP and access was taken up at the Fourth Ministerial Conference, held at Doha, Qatar. These discussions produced the Doha declaration of 2001. While the TRIPS Agreement had included some safeguards that countries could invoke to make IP enforcement adaptable to public health needs, the Doha declaration clarified lingering ambiguities surrounding these provisions. It made clear the legality and legitimacy of measures like the granting of compulsory licenses, whereby, when faced with a public health emergency, governments can legally circumvent a patent to either produce a drug themselves or authorize a generic producer to do so. It also took up the question of parallel importation, whereby countries lacking the capacity to manufacture a needed generic within their territory might import it from abroad. And it extended the grace period allowed to least developed countries for the implementation of TRIPS provisions, granting them until 2016 to become fully compliant.

Defenders of the hegemonic approach to intellectual property, of course, insist that claims of an inherent conflict between enhanced IP protections and access to medicines are overblown. They don't deny that access to medicines is a problem, but they attribute blame to social forces like poverty and the lack of access to health services in many countries. They prefer to address access problems through preferential pricing (a process whereby drug companies voluntarily offer lower price drugs to health systems in poor countries) or donations, which are often administered through private foundations. This way, access is broadened for poor patients without altering the incentive structure at the heart of the patent system.

Indeed, to tinker with the system itself by invoking things like compulsory licensing is dangerous, intellectual property advocates argue. For example, as the U.S. Chamber of Commerce's Global Intellectual Property Center warns,

> Even as some nations are taking steps to improve IP rights, a range of anti-IP NGOs [nongovernmental organizations] are working—often through multilateral organizations such as the World Health Organization—to undermine respect for IP. These groups, which include not only relatively new NGOs but also some of America's oldest foundations, have launched an anti-IP campaign built around access. They believe that no matter how much has been invested in research and development and individual risk taking and hard work, the world should have virtually free and open access to new drugs, breakthrough technologies, and artistic creations. . . . Should these activists prevail, there would be fewer resources available for medical and technological advances that save lives and raise living standards worldwide. Their agenda is to take property away from those who create and own it without just compensation or the rule of reasonable law. They

see IP as a problem when it is, in fact, a solution to many of the challenges facing society. (Global Intellectual Property Center n/d, 15–16)

In response to access advocates' successes in the South African case and at Doha, advocates of a maximalist IP agenda have pursued their policies through other venues. As Sell (2010) and Drahos (2007) illustrate, the continuous upward ratchet of IP protection has been made possible by a complex and coordinated set of strategies pursued simultaneously in multiple fora. This "forum shopping" has been key to their success. For example, under Section 301 of the Trade Act of 1974, amended in 1988, the office of the U.S. trade representative conducts an annual review of foreign countries' IP policies, placing those deemed to have serious IP rights deficiencies on a watch list or priority watch list. U.S. companies can request countries' placement on these lists, exposing them to the risk of trade sanctions or retaliation at the WTO. According to Sell (2003), between 1996 and 2000 most countries wound up on the watch lists at the instigation of PhRMA. In this way, countries can be placed on the list even if their IP policies are fully compliant with international law but run afoul of the private preferences of U.S. corporations. And, once on the list, bilateral relationships between countries can expose targeted nations to all sorts of public and behind-the-scenes pressure to alter their policies. Countries that are highly dependent on the United States, like those of Central America, are particularly vulnerable to such incentives.

Other tactics include the growing securitization of IP discourse, as more aggressive intellectual property policies are advocated on the grounds that this will combat not only counterfeiting but terrorism (Sell 2010). In September 2001, just weeks after the attacks in New York and Washington, former Clinton administration IP lawyer Roslyn Mazer published an op-ed in *The Washington Post* warning of the links between IP violations and terrorism:

> Recent developments suggest that many of the governments suspected of supporting al Qaeda are also promoting, being corrupted by, or at the very least ignoring highly lucrative trafficking in counterfeit and pirated products capable of generating huge money flows to terrorists and other organized criminal groups . . . The convergence of our economic security and our national security became starkly apparent on Sept. 11. The staggering

economic losses to America's copyright and trademark industries—alarming unto themselves—now are compounded by the opportunistic trafficking in IP products to finance terrorism and other organized criminal endeavors. (Mazer 2001, 2)

Although such arguments are thin on evidence, their advancement through closed-door discussions about national security makes them difficult to contest. Indeed, in 2009, as the United States and the governments of dozens of countries were engaged in the negotiations over the Anti-Counterfeiting Trade Agreement, or ACTA, activists sought access to a copy of the proposed text of the agreement by filing a Freedom of Information Act request. The Obama administration responded that the text of the agreement was classified, for revealing its content could be prejudicial to national security (Love 2009).

And lastly, intellectual property maximalists have ratcheted up standards through the inclusion of "TRIPS-plus" provisions in bilateral trade agreements between the United States or European Union and weaker countries. Central America's experience with CAFTA is a textbook example of this strategy. If mobilization against the IP agenda at the WTO was challenging for access to medicines activists, responding to this multi-pronged assault is infinitely more so. Opposing new standards in bilateral trade deals like CAFTA is a daunting task for grassroots activists: Rather than a single standard arrived at through public deliberations among nations, deals are struck behind closed doors and disputes resolved through private arbitration. What's more, civil societies in the affected countries are often ill informed about technical points of trade law, and because deals are bilateral the ability to join forces in coalitions of Global South countries is limited. Government negotiators, too, face formidable challenges given the overwhelming imbalance of power between poor countries and the United States. And the conditioning of trade agreements on the adoption of IP chapters pits health advocates against other, often powerful sectors within developing countries who stand to benefit from trade agreements and therefore advocate forcefully for their approval.

In this context, organizing in the human rights tradition to contest hegemonic interpretations of IP faces formidable challenges. In some ways, I argue that intellectual property presents a test case of sorts, through which we can see how effective human rights institutions and arguments might be at tackling the political-economic terrain they have increasingly claimed for themselves. Are we really up to the challenge?

IP's Challenge to Human Rights

When my students and I returned from meeting Edgar in Guatemala in 2004, we did our best to inform others about the impact CAFTA could have on people like him. We wrote op-ed articles, spoke at conferences, attended meetings, and shared their stories with anyone willing to listen. Months later, in early 2005, I received a phone call from a member of the *New York Times* editorial board, who was considering writing an editorial on this topic. Instantly, my heart leaped into my mouth. All those interviews with AIDS patients—this was my chance to honor the hope they held (vainly, I'd always feared) that in telling me their story, I might carry it with me and share it in a way that might change something. Yet . . .

"What's going to be the body count?" she asked bluntly, cutting through my long-winded explanation of the IP mechanisms contained in the agreement. And I didn't have an answer. After all, as mentioned earlier, measuring intellectual property's impact is not as straightforward as it might seem. Because IP rules delay the entrance of generic versions of new drugs, their impact is only gradually felt as new drugs become available without generic alternatives. But no one is wresting pills out of poor patients' clenched fists; dispassionate bureaucratic decisions mean prices will stay higher, longer, but most patients will be given an older drug or prescribed an alternate therapy, rather than denied treatment altogether. There are likely to be patients who receive a less than ideal therapy and programs for which there are fewer funds because more is spent on medicines, but most likely there will never be a quantifiable "body count."

This doesn't mean the impact of intellectual property is insignificant; far from it. Rather, it means IP poses important new challenges for human rights advocates. While skyrocketing prices in state drug purchasing programs are certainly a problem, it's hard to identify specific "victims" of intellectual property—the prototypical patient who died because she didn't get her drugs. Yet we know from past research that rights campaigns work best when they highlight identifiable and "innocent" victims, when the abuse in question is violent, and when the responsible party is willfully ruthless. The quiet, impersonal, almost indiscernible narrowing of health care options that IP brings about through a thousand bureaucratic decisions is harder to contest through the familiar "naming and shaming" tactics of human rights campaigns. It's vitally important, therefore, that we develop new tools to conduct this work, not only for practical purposes—to ensure that Edgar and others like him get the medicine they need—but for political ones of far broader relevance; for ensuring fairness in trade rules is ever more central to the global struggle for human rights.

While the idea of social and economic rights remains novel in the United States, a number of Southern Hemisphere states have committed themselves to the concept, inscribing such rights in their constitutions and dedicating institutional resources to their enforcement. Courts from South Africa to India to Brazil have upheld such rights. Human rights organizations—even the slow-to-move titans like Amnesty—are today campaigning on a wider range of issues than ever before, including especially the right to health, a centerpiece of Amnesty's current "Demand Dignity" campaign. And such work has begun to enable us to frame not only dictators' dirty deeds, but the injustices embedded in our trade regimes, as rights abuses.

Yet human rights tactics are still drawn from a tool kit first developed to stop civil and political rights abuses, and all the research about when the "boomerang" works best still suggests that they are most effective when deployed against cases conforming to a certain narrow register. How do we advocate for rights without identifiable victims, without rapacious dictators, without a quantifiable "body count"? How do we render economic decision making in rights terms? The answers to these questions are of vital tactical importance in evolving struggles for global justice.

And, on a more theoretical level, intellectual property battles offer important insights in the struggle for global human rights, though they pose challenges too. On the one hand, Northern corporations' battles to secure IP interests in areas where markets for their products are miniscule may appear puzzling. Why fight so hard for a prize so small? Yet in fact, I argue, the struggle is not for market share—at least not in the tiny markets of Central America—but for precedent. Is health a human right or a commodity? Writ larger, to what extent should public welfare trump private profit? The debate about intellectual property is fundamentally a debate about the place of the market in social life. This is arguably the central debate political philosophers have entertained since at least Adam Smith, but it has particular resonance in our times, after decades of designing social policy in market-centered terms.

For advocates of "free" trade, intellectual property protection is bedrock. Although a relative latecomer to the "free" trade pantheon, its successful positioning as a form of property and of its opponents as lawless miscreants ("pirates") binds it to the core values of the field. To surrender such terrain could suggest the relativism of other core principles of free enterprise; to do so would be anathema.

For advocates of human rights and global justice, too, IP represents a direct strike at the core of the movement's principles. While numerous elements of contemporary trade agreements evoke activist ire, perhaps no other element crystallizes the contradiction between "free" trade and global justice as clearly as intellectual property. Progressives certainly criticize recent U.S. trade agreements on other counts—for failing to address poor countries' records of weak respect for labor rights or environmental protection, for example—but the chief complaint there is that the agreements allow an intolerable situation to persist. In the case of IP, the agreements go a step further, introducing *new* rights claims that threaten to make the existing situation worse.[4] What's more, the threat strikes directly at the right to life, the hallowed core from which other rights spring. The incursion of IP in trade agreements thus represents a bald assertion that private monopoly rights of North American corporations merit protection even at the cost of poor people's lives. For those who see multiple injustices in the current trade regime, to fail to contest this ultimate affront would be to concede everything.

We should not imagine this as a struggle between those "for" and "against" globalization: Both sides of this argument advocate visions of a highly complex and interconnected world. On the one side, the governments of the United States and the European Union, and the corporations whose officers advise them, have staked all trade discussions on the adoption of enhanced IP protections, insisting that such measures are necessary components of global commerce. On the other, a growing band of activists has framed their opposition to intellectual property in terms of international human rights obligations and has formulated campaigns using transnational alliances for open access.

The question, then, is not whether globalization is "good" or "bad," nor is it whether one favors the "global" or "local," or the "North" or "South," but on what specific terms—according to whose rules, at the service of which ideals—our already globalized world is to conduct its business. If IP law's specific tenets are esoteric, its implications should be broadly examined, for it is precisely in these technicalities of transnational trade law that globalization's rule book is being written.

Chapter 3

Market Failures and Fallacies

D R. EDUARDO ARATHOON SERVES AS DIRECTOR of Guatemala's only HIV/AIDS specialist clinic. He works half-days in private practice to pay the bills, but his heart lies in the Clínica Familiar Luis Ángel García, where he spends his mornings tending to AIDS patients, most too poor to afford medicine, many shunned by their families for having acquired a deeply stigmatized illness. He patches together treatments from donations and works out ways to enroll his patients in clinical trials[1] so they can receive drugs. A few years ago, Dr. Arathoon's clinic held a lottery for medicines: Those patients who drew the lucky numbers received the antiretroviral drugs necessary to keep them alive; those who didn't, didn't (Zarembo 1999, 25).

In the United States, where HIV has become a treatable, if not curable, illness, changes in prescriptions are common as doctors, and patients work to constantly adjust their treatment regimen to their body's shifting needs. So a few years ago, Dr. Arathoon and a U.S. physician friend worked out a plan. In New York, patients could return their unused pills to his clinic, where they'd be packed up and sent south with traveling friends—a few dozen here, a couple hundred there. The scheme kept Dr. Arathoon's patients alive, while it lasted, but once the laws on drug trafficking got stricter, it became untenable. Of course, one could argue there is something disturbing about Dr. Arathoon and his colleagues piecing together treatment for poor patients on drugs originally prescribed to others; this is prohibited in the United States. But, on the other hand, there is something more disturbing about following all the rules to let them die.

As regards health and intellectual property, Central America is a place of contradictions. Health indicators across the region—with the notable exception of Costa Rica—testify to high levels of deaths from preventable illness, malnutrition, and other maladies; public health services are underfunded and overburdened; state hospitals often lack medicine, and stories of waiting for months for treatment are not uncommon.

Yet despite this dismal record, Central American societies have been leaders in defining health as a human right. And now, they are leaders— or laggards, depending on one's point of view—in offering some of the world's highest standards of intellectual property protection. Of course, these promises contain paradoxes: It's hard to imagine how countries that commit in their constitutions to uphold the human right to health, serving populations where most patients live on less than $2 a day, could make good on these pledges without relying heavily on the use of generic drugs. And yet the intellectual property standards in CAFTA threaten to constrict access to generic drugs over time, for reasons explained in Chapter 2. How will countries balance these contending commitments?

On the one hand, at the level of core concepts, intellectual property poses a simple trade-off—as Stiglitz says, it's life versus profits (Stiglitz 2006)—but, on the other, it's an enormously complex empirical challenge to marshal the data that would enable the framing of economic decisions in human rights terms. And how we measure it matters, as I argue in this chapter. After first providing an overview of the area's major health challenges and the history of institutional efforts to ameliorate them, I explain CAFTA's IP provisions, illustrating how in many cases national implementing legislation goes beyond the requirements of the agreement itself. This raises many concerns about CAFTA's likely impact on access to medicines. Yet, as I go on to argue, measuring this impact is extraordinarily complex. While various methodologies have been used to gauge the impact of intellectual property on access to medicines, I argue that most give us only a partial picture of what should be human rights advocates' paramount concern: whether real patients get the drugs they need.

For obvious—and appropriate—reasons, most impact studies have focused on drug prices as the site at which IP's impact is expected to be found. Yet in this chapter I argue that, while drug pricing is a vitally important piece of the puzzle, scholars and practitioners interested in the right to health must look beyond price points to examine the actual functioning of markets, to look at the way prices and public decision making intersect. Ultimately, prices reflect market realities with which responsible policy makers must grapple, but it is in this grappling process, not in the prices themselves, that the right to health is upheld or violated. To understand IP's impact therefore requires a holistic view of the interlocking nexus between state decision making, market forces, patient advocacy, and private profiteering.

Sickness and Health in Central America

Enjoyment of the right to health faces fundamental challenges in Central America. As is typical of poor countries, the nations of Central America, with the exception of Costa Rica, are plagued with high levels of preventable illness. Outside Costa Rica, for example, approximately 12 to 13 percent of deaths of Central American children under age five are still attributable to diarrheal disease (World Health Organization 2010). Chronic malnutrition is also a problem; in Guatemala, for example, stunting affected as much as 54.3 percent of the population under five years of age in 2002, although other countries had considerably lower rates (World Health Organization 2010). Despite this, many health indicators have improved significantly in recent decades, as shown in Table 3.1. Mortality rates of infants and children under five have decreased across the region, in some cases quite dramatically; El Salvador, for example, reduced its infant mortality by more than half between 1990 and 2006 (World Health Organization 2010). Maternal mortality rates have also decreased, although countries like Guatemala (at 290 deaths per 100,000 live births) and Honduras (at 280) still report rates much higher than the Latin American average (World Health Organization 2010). And life expectancies at birth have steadily climbed for both women and men.

Across the region today, classic health problems associated with poverty and underdevelopment coexist with patterns of disease more typical of the developed world. Public health scholars refer to this situation as a double burden of disease, common as poor countries undergo the so-called epidemiological transition to the afflictions of the affluent world. In

TABLE 3.1   Health indicators in Central America.

	Costa Rica	El Salvador	Guatemala	Honduras	Nicaragua
Infant mortality rate per 1000 live births (1990/2006)	16/11	47/22	60/31	45/23	52/29
Life expectancy at birth, both sexes (1990/2006)	76/78	65/71	63/68	66/70	67/71
Per capita government expenditure on health, in USD (2006)	$264	$113	$54	$47	$42
Access to antiretroviral therapy among people with advanced HIV (2006)	>95%	46%	31%	41%	26%

Source: World Health Organization 2010.

Guatemala, for example, the Pan American Health Organization reported in 2007 that "the number of deaths due to communicable diseases has decreased from 76 to 62% of total recorded deaths; however, deaths from cardiovascular diseases have increased by 61% and from tumors by 100% during the same period" (Pan American Health Organization 2007, 12). Similarly, rates of diabetes and other chronic, noncommunicable diseases associated with urban lifestyles and diets high in saturated fats and sugars are on the rise. This poses important challenges for health systems, and particularly for access to medicines, as patients with chronic diseases typically require more expensive therapies sustained over a longer period of time; by contrast, most (though not all) infectious diseases can be treated cheaply with drugs whose patents have long ago expired. In Central America, the purchase of medicines typically constitutes countries' second largest health expenditure after the payment of health workers' salaries, and drug costs are expected only to climb as the population ages and the incidence of chronic diseases increases.

Of course, some infectious diseases, like HIV, do require very expensive treatment sustained over time. The UNAIDS Global Report 2010 estimates that less than 1 percent of the region's population in the fifteen to forty-nine year age range lives with HIV/AIDS; in Costa Rica and Nicaragua, rates are estimated below 0.5 percent (UNAIDS 2010). Compared to sub-Saharan Africa, this represents a relatively low burden of disease, although it is among the higher rates in Latin America. Access to antiretroviral treatment is quite poor: Among people with advanced HIV infections, coverage is estimated at higher than 95 percent for Costa Rica but only 46 percent for El Salvador, 31 percent for Guatemala, 41 percent for Honduras, and 26 percent for Nicaragua (World Health Organization 2010). These numbers are all the more sobering when taken in light of the most recent research showing that early (and even prophylactic) provision of antiretrovirals significantly inhibits the transmission of the virus. In other words, if we know that early treatment saves lives, more meaningful measures of access would include people with less advanced stages of the virus, producing coverage rates even lower than those reported in the preceding paragraph.

In this context, then, access to medicines is a growing area of concern for Central American health advocates. In recent years, increasing attention has been paid to the question of when and why health systems do such a poor job of ensuring access.

Health Rights and Institutions in Central America

Despite a long history of officially regarding health as a human right, Central American health systems are deeply inequitable, and in many cases they fail dramatically to deliver on this promise. Through the years, there have been various attempts to remedy this, including at least three significant periods of change in the twentieth century. First, in the 1940s, social security institutes were established to protect workers and their families; second, in the 1960s and 1970s, governments implemented—although imperfectly—new primary health care policies promoted by the Pan-American Health Organization; and lastly, in the 1980s and 1990s, governments turned away from this model to adopt structural reforms favored by the World Bank and Inter-American Development Bank. Throughout these periods, as I explore in more detail in Chapter 4, progressive health activists associated with the tradition of Latin American social medicine advocated a vision of health rooted in human rights, community participation, and preventative approaches, as opposed to the physician-centered, curative model more familiar in biomedicine.

Most Central American states did not begin to invest significantly in health until after World War II. In the mid-twentieth century, new public health systems were among the hallmarks of a period characterized by a flourishing of social democracy across Latin America. During this period, Latin American countries embraced the ideal of the state as an arbiter of social justice rather than simply a narrow guarantor of individual rights (Grandin 2005, 46–67; Grandin 2004). Latin American constitutions from this era reflect this expansive vision in their extensive treatment of labor rights, public education, and social security. Indeed, a number of scholars have noted the prominence afforded to social and economic rights by Latin American delegates to the deliberations that produced the Universal Declaration of Human Rights, arguing that far from simply derivative of Northern models, Latin American Constitutionalism responded to its own distinctive amalgam of intellectual and political traditions (Wright-Carozza 2003, 281; Glendon 2003, 27)

Health rights constitute a particularly prominent component of this vision. Not only were health rights recognized in the region's constitutions, but institutions were created to provide for their fulfillment. Costa Rica's constitution is the only one in Central America that does not explicitly recognize the right to health, though it grants many associated rights, and subsequent jurisprudence has constructed the right to health from the right to life. Particularly significant was the establishment of social security systems in 1942 in Costa Rica, in 1946 in Guatemala, and in 1949 in El Salvador.

Although these represented important steps toward universal access, most Central American resources for health were still allocated in such a way as to reflect and reaffirm the deeply unequal social structures characteristic of the region. The establishment of social security in Central America created dual health systems, in which resources were divided between the Ministry of Health, intended to provide services to all citizens, and social security institutes, designed to cover formal sector employees and their dependents (Palmer 2005, 59) To complicate the picture yet further, in some cases separate institutions were established to tend to the needs of specific populations, such as the military or teachers. In Costa Rica, reforms were introduced early on to combat this fragmentation of the health system; today, as a result, the Ministry of Health serves a regulatory function, but virtually all state expenditures on health are allocated to the country's social security system, the Caja Costarricense de Seguridad Social, which provides treatment to everyone within the national territory. In Guatemala and El Salvador, however, health systems remain characterized by high degrees of fragmentation,[2] with policies, budgets, and patients spread across a range of institutions.

This fragmentation has important implications for the right to health, as the different budgetary allocations for each institution permit different levels of care. In many cases, social security institutes, which outside of Costa Rica attend only those employed in the formal sector, enjoy more resources per patient than other institutions. In Guatemala, for example, the social security institute, IGSS, covers approximately 11 percent of the population. Yet the Pan American Health Organization reports that "a comparative analysis of per capita spending in the public sub-sector in 2005 shows that the Ministry of Health spent US$32.22 per inhabitant and the IGSS spent US$298" (Pan American Health Organization 2007, 35). IGSS affiliates are already drawn from a disproportionately privileged segment of the population—as salaried formal sector employees, they tend to hail from urban, middle-class, nonindigenous backgrounds (Centro de Investigaciones Económicas Nacionales [CIEN] 2006)—and through IGSS they have access to higher quality care, thus exacerbating existing inequalities.

Institutional drug purchasing practices vary by country, though all have open bidding processes for drug procurement and official policies that mandate preferential purchase of lower-cost generics, where they can be shown to be safe and effective.[3] Given the lack of effective government testing of the drug supply, however, different institutions use different criteria to assess the safety and efficacy of generics. In Costa Rica, the Caja maintains a basic list of approved medications and concentrates its purchase of these drugs to obtain the lowest prices. In Guatemala, the IGSS and Ministry of Health have separate drug lists, but all purchasing is conducted through a single government procurement system, Guatecompras. In El Salvador, there is no unitary process for drug procurement, and each institution (ISSS [Instituto Salvadoreño del Seguro Social], Ministry of Health, and health systems for teachers and the military) maintains separate lists. In all cases, cost effectiveness is among the criteria for a drug's inclusion in the basic list, though different institutions assess it differently.

Intellectual Property Comes to Central America

New Rules for the Region

Intellectual property norms first arrived in Central America via the requirements countries had acquired, by virtue of their membership in the WTO, to implement TRIPS; the rules were later made more aggressive through the "TRIPS-plus" demands of CAFTA and were subsequently ratcheted up yet further in the process of formulating national law, which sometimes exceeds CAFTA standards. These three "ratchets" did not always occur sequentially; sometimes, for example, national legislatures passed aggressive CAFTA-plus standards into law prior to the ratification of the agreement itself, though such developments were clearly motivated by the overall context of the treaty's negotiation. Nor did the three ratchets occur in isolation: In fact, because TRIPS includes a requirement of most favored nation treatment—whereby any advantages granted by a WTO member state to nationals of another country must also be granted to the nationals of all WTO member states—when Central American countries "voluntarily" accede to TRIPS-plus protections in an agreement with the United States or EU, they automatically agree to those same protections in virtually all of their trade relationships (Drahos 2007, 11), so policy that gets made bilaterally effectively becomes global policy.

But this is an important though in some ways counterintuitive point: Though the impetus for intellectual property in Central America clearly came from the global North, the most dangerous strains of the disease developed locally. To be sure, these initiatives were clearly advocated by individuals and institutions with inextricable ties to Northern corporations and/or governments, but they reached their most extreme manifestation in local laws. Ultimately, this suggests the need to move beyond understandings of these processes rooted in a global/local binary, approaching them instead as transnational, multisited struggles characterized by enormous differences in power and access to information at each site. I will return to this point later, after offering an overview of the history and implications of intellectual property in Central America.

Prior to the passage of TRIPS in 1994, there was little effective protection for intellectual property in Central America. As regards pharmaceuticals, only Costa Rica and El Salvador had any patent laws on the books, though their short patent terms, small markets, and lax enforcement meant that few companies bothered to seek patents in the region. Under the terms of TRIPS, Central American countries were granted a five-year transition period to become IP compliant or face WTO sanctions; as a result, most countries of the region introduced legislation in late 1999 and early 2000. The bulk of the 2000-era reforms were limited to introducing the twenty-year patent term and the figure of test data protection (although in El Salvador and Costa Rica, consistent with the text of TRIPS, no set term was established for test data protection). Guatemala, on the other hand, in an apparent bid to demonstrate its eagerness to play nice with transnational capital, passed a law in 2000 establishing fifteen years of test data exclusivity, then the longest period of such protection offered by any country in the world.

Despite this, the issue of intellectual property and access to medicines did not begin to attract widespread public attention in Central America until 2003 at the earliest—even in Guatemala, where in early 2003 the data protection law was quietly repealed at the instigation of local generics producers. Closed-door negotiations for CAFTA began in that year, although the text of the agreement was not made public until early 2004.

CAFTA's intellectual property rules are very complex; limited space precludes a full explanation here. Yet, in very general terms, they might be grouped into two categories: monopoly expanding and responsibility shifting. I discuss each of these, briefly, in the following paragraphs.

First, CAFTA *extends the monopoly provisions* contained in TRIPS. CAFTA mandates the extension of patent protection beyond the twenty-year term established in TRIPS, to compensate for "unreasonable" procedural delays (either in granting patents, [Article 15.9.6a] or in securing marketing approval for pharmaceuticals [Article 15.9.6b]). And as regards test data protection, CAFTA introduces a number of important new details that expand its monopoly-making impact. First, CAFTA mandates a minimum of five years for test data protection, where TRIPS leaves the protection period open to interpretation. Second, where TRIPS mandates the application of test data protection to new chemical entities, CAFTA mandates its application to new products—a broader category, thus casting the monopoly net wider. And lastly, CAFTA expands the concept of test data protection into test data *exclusivity.* TRIPS Article 39.1 discusses "protection against unfair competition" but does not mandate exclusivity; a state could choose to interpret this mandate in ways that still allow generic competition by recognizing it as fair. Argentina, in fact, has followed such a path. Under CAFTA, on the other hand, no such judgment is left open to the state; not simply protection, but exclusivity, is required (Correa 2006a).

And second, in a departure from TRIPS, CAFTA *tasks states with enforcing private rights.* This is achieved through the introduction of mechanisms such as "linkage," whereby drug regulatory offices are mandated to ensure that products they license are in full compliance with intellectual property law. This saddles drug regulatory authorities with a task they are neither trained nor funded to do; under previous patent systems, and indeed under U.S. law, it falls to private IP holders to detect any infringement of their patent and take such cases to court. Under CAFTA, this responsibility falls to the state—and the sanctions contemplated are criminal in addition to civil. Thus, critics charge, states shoulder new responsibilities, and face new potential sanctions should they fail to comply (Correa 2006b, 399).

National Implementation

Scholars and activists alike have largely ignored implementation questions—and for access advocates, we do so at our peril. As Peter Drahos (2007) has warned, even apparent victories in pushing for access-friendly IP law at the international level mean little if states fail to put them into practice. Yet, as Carolyn Deere writes, discussing TRIPS implementation, "To date, WTO scholars have generally examined implementation from a legal or descriptive perspective, overlooking the ways in which it is a dynamic political process and the scope for different interpretations of legal commitments" (2009, 21). Unfortunately, in the Central American case, as discussed in Chapter 4, all the transnational campaigning focused on agreement ratification, and, although written guidelines were prepared to assist countries in crafting responsible implementation legislation,[4] there were no powerful political coalitions in place to push this issue. Unlike, for example, India (see Kapczynski 2009), Central American nations were not proactive in seeking creative interpretations of TRIPS requirements that might favor national interests.

Alejandro Cerón and I conducted a survey of domestic intellectual property legislation before and after CAFTA's passage as a way of assessing the changes wrought by the agreement (Cerón and Godoy 2009, 787). The findings for Costa Rica, El Salvador, and Guatemala are summarized in Table 3.2, using a framework proposed by Chaves and Olivera for measuring the compatibility of IP legislation with public health concerns across

TABLE 3.2 Public health sensitivity of domestic IP legislation, before and after CAFTA.

	Before/after CAFTA?	Opportunities						Threats					
		Patentability exemptions	*Bolar-type exception*	*Other exceptions to patent rights*	*Parallel importation*	*Grounds for compulsory license*	*Grounds for government use*	*Patent extension*	*Linkage*	*Data protection*	*"New product" definition*	*Grace period*	*"New uses" protection*
Costa Rica	pre	+	+	+	0	+	+	0	0	+	0	0	0
	post	+	0	0	0	+	+	–	–	–	–	0	0
El Salvador	pre	+	0	–	0	+	0	0	0	+	0	0	0
	post	+	+	–	0	+	0	–	–	–	–	–	0
Guatemala	pre	+	0	+	0	+	+	0	0	-	0	0	0
	post	+	+	+	0	+	+	–	–	–	–	–	+

+ TRIPS flexibility or the TRIPS Plus provision allows an interpretation that privileges breaking the IP protection for public health needs.

0 TRIPS flexibility or TRIPS Plus provision is not explicitly included in the legislation.

– TRIPS flexibility or the TRIPS Plus provision privileges the intellectual property protection even if it confronts public health needs.

Source: Adapted from Cerón and Godoy 2009, 787.

countries (Chaves and Oliveira 2007, 49). This approach identifies both opportunities and threats that national implementation may introduce—things like the incorporation of TRIPS flexibilities into national law, thus presumably making them easier to invoke later on (an opportunity) or the adoption of patent extensions (a threat). As can be seen in Table 3.2, considerable variation exists across Central American countries, despite the fact that all were responding to a uniform text. Furthermore, the passage of CAFTA led to the incorporation of numerous threats to public health.

Worse yet, however, in several instances countries went beyond the requirements of the agreement, introducing "CAFTA-plus" threats. This is not altogether uncommon, as Deere's global survey shows (2009). For example, TRIPS established a twenty-year patent term but did not contemplate the extension of patents beyond this duration. As already noted, CAFTA took a step further, mandating the extension of patents beyond the twenty-year term in circumstances where "unreasonable" delays were incurred in the process of patent concession or the granting of marketing approval (CAFTA Article 15.9.6). Yet the affected countries have chosen to interpret this mandate differently: Costa Rica and El Salvador stipulate a maximum extension of eighteen months, the Dominican Republic stipulates a maximum of three years, and Guatemala included no such limit whatsoever on the duration of the extension.

As already noted, article 39.3 of TRIPS mandates test data protection for new chemical entities, whereas CAFTA mandates protection for "new products." The difference is significant; the meaning of "new chemical entities" has been hotly debated in a number of contexts, including most notably the discussions surrounding the 2005 reforms to India's patent law. Yet CAFTA introduces a new category—that of *new products*, defined as: "A new product is one that does not contain a chemical entity that has been previously approved" in the country (Article 15.10:1[c]). Effectively, this broadens the category of products to which test data protection must be applied to include compounds that contain a mixture of new and previously known substances (Correa 2006a). But this apparently slight difference matters, as a number of new drugs on the market are compounds involving previously marketed substances; this is particularly the case with second-line antiretroviral treatments for HIV/AIDS.

Costa Rica

Guatemala and El Salvador

FIGURE 3.1. Definition in force in Costa Rica (requires no test data protection for compound substances with previously known components) and Guatemala and El Salvador (requires test data protection for compound substances with previously known components).

The language in Costa Rica's implementation legislation mirrors that of CAFTA, defining a new product as one that "does not contain a chemical entity that has been previously approved in Costa Rica" (Asamblea Legislativa de la Republica de Costa Rica 2000 Art 8). Yet Guatemalan and Salvadoran legislation stipulates that a new product is one "which contains a chemical entity not previously approved in the country" (Congreso de la República de Guatemala 2005). In the original Spanish, the distinction between the Costa Rican and Guatemalan/Salvadoran definitions is merely the placement of the word "no" at different points in the same sentence.

As Figure 3.1 illustrates, under the definition of a "new product" applied in Costa Rica, a drug that combines a previously recognized substance and a new one—such as Abbott's Kaletra, recognized as an essential medicine by WHO—would not be eligible for test data protection. Under the definition in force in Guatemala, however, such a product would be granted a five-year market monopoly.

Moving Beyond the Law on the Books:
Assessing CAFTA's Impact

If, despite arising from a uniform text, CAFTA's implementation legislation varies widely across countries (Godoy and Cerón 2011, 1186), we should expect another layer of variable interpretations to color the way each country's legislation is applied in practice. And this is the key human rights question: not just what the laws on the books say but how they can be expected to impact real people's lives. Yet conducting empirical assessments of the agreement's actual impact on health is a much more challenging task, for a number of reasons. To begin with, even in its most aggressive formulations, IP's impact should be gradual and staggered rather than instantaneous or across-the-board: intellectual property delays generics' entry to market, but this only becomes relevant to health when a new drug is developed, a Central American country wants to purchase it, and generics are not yet allowed because of IP. As such, many factors mediate IP's impact on health, including the extent to which new, therapeutically important drugs are being introduced; the interest of Central American states in buying these drugs; and the speed with which one calculates such drugs would have hit the market in generic form absent IP protection. And of course, all of these mediating factors are at least as subject to political forces as they are economic principles; as Drahos warns, "More important than the rules of international law are the politics" (Drahos 2007, 23–24).

Recognizing the possibility of such varied interpretations—and at the same time the imperative of deriving sound estimates to guide policy making—a consortium of organizations including WHO, the Pan American Health Organization, the UN Development Programme (UNDP), the World Bank Institute (WBI) and the International Centre for Trade and Sustainable Development (ICTSD) have developed a complex econometric methodology for projecting the impact of intellectual property based on four scenarios of varying severity (Rovira, Abbas, and Cortés 2009). In Central America, this model has only been applied the case of Costa Rica (Hernández-González and Valverde 2009). Significantly, even under the baseline scenario, that of TRIPS requirements alone (in other words, a "CAFTA-minus" scenario), the authors predicted rising costs due to growing monopoly conditions in the medicines market. Under the most unfavorable scenario, the authors predicted the social security institute would need to increase its budget for medicines by US$331 million by 2030 and that some 28 percent of drugs would enjoy monopoly access to the Costa Rican market by that year (compared to 12 percent under a "CAFTA-minus" scenario) (Hernández-González and Valverde 2009).

IP and the Dual Fiction of Drug Markets

However, data derived from pricing measures do not automatically answer human rights questions. Indeed, as I insist in the following discussion, while fulfilling the right to health undeniably requires grappling with economic realities—and skyrocketing drug prices clearly represent one of the chief challenges to sustainable health systems—understanding how changing IP policies produce or constrict enjoyment of the right to health requires examining these forces in their broader sociopolitical context. Too often, intellectual property analyses conclude by demonstrating that a given set of drug prices (produced under monopoly conditions conferred by IP protection) vastly exceeds the prices available for the same drugs in other markets without IP constraints; from this, authors infer that IP is the obstacle to competition and oppose it in the name of access to medicines. I do not dispute the basic premise that intellectual property, in blocking competition, can be an impediment to access. But I worry that in leaving our arguments there[5]—as a call to reject IP because it is a barrier to competition—we may unwittingly reinscribe notions about the virtues of the self-regulating market in ways that ultimately undermine our cause.[6]

In fact, markets are social constructs, not "natural" forces. And we already know that, in human rights terms, the market for pharmaceuticals has failed—so we should be wary of basing our access arguments on propping it up. In the following pages, I suggest that it has failed in at least two ways. Neither of these are my own unique insights; they are already-documented "inconvenient truths" that have yet to be incorporated in discussions around the impact of intellectual property. They raise important questions.

First, as has been amply demonstrated elsewhere, market-driven innovation has led to a profound disconnect between public health needs and pharmaceutical research and development; to put it more bluntly, the market spits out a lot of unnecessary drugs. Should human rights advocates care that the latest "me-too" drug is IP protected? Second, even without IP there is very little competition in many drug markets; at least in Central America, competition is not a "natural" fact, nor does it always effectively reduce prices. Is it enough, therefore, to argue that intellectual property impedes access? I argue that these two questions can be answered only by examining the sociopolitical context in which decisions are made about drug purchasing. After explaining these two market fallacies, I share the stories of two drugs in Guatemala as case studies of these dynamics.

Fallacy #1: Drug Markets Are Innovative

For all the discussion about market-driven "innovation," it bears remembering that much of what originator pharmaceutical companies have produced in recent years is not particularly innovative, at least in therapeutic terms. In 2003, the U.S. FDA concluded that while the pharmaceutical industry had been seeking the approval of a greater number of drugs in recent years, a decreasing percentage of that pool represented truly innovative products (U.S. Food and Drug Administration 2003). Similarly, a GAO (Government Accountability Office) review of FDA data from 1993 through 2005 found that most of the new products approved by the FDA were in fact modifications to existing drugs; indeed, 68 percent of new drug applications were classified by the FDA as modifications of existing drugs (U.S. Government Accountability Office 2006). Marcia Angell and other scholars have written extensively about the pharmaceutical industry's production of these so-called me-too drugs, which represent little to no therapeutic gain for patients but allow the industry to patent new products and benefit from market monopolies even when existing drugs on the market are just as good and in most cases less costly (Angell 2004).

One of the most frequently cited examples is AstraZeneca's Nexium, a heartburn drug that was introduced just as the patent on AstraZeneca's blockbuster drug Prilosec was set to expire in 2001. While Prilosec contains two isomers of omeprazole, Nexium contains just one, making it, according to Marcia Angell, essentially "half of Prilosec"; so far, no scientific evidence has demonstrated that this is better for patients. Yet when AstraZeneca introduced Nexium it rolled out an elaborate marketing campaign that rapidly made "the little purple pill" the most heavily advertised drug in the United States (Angell 2004). Prilosec is now sold over the counter for a fraction of the price of Nexium, yet many patients and doctors were persuaded by the marketing campaign to switch to the more expensive alternative, Nexium.

In Guatemala, Nexium currently enjoys the platinum standard in test data protection: fifteen years. But generic versions of Prilosec are available for a fraction of the cost. If our primary preoccupation is with human rights, not with market access for generics, should it matter that Guatemalans seeking Nexium must pay premium prices?

Existing impact assessment studies approach the me-too problem in two ways. Some studies seek only to measure the aggregate impact of intellectual property protection on the market as a whole, thus demonstrating higher costs across the board, without differentiating between innovative therapies and me-toos. Others, seeking to limit information to drugs of public health significance, examine the impact of IP only on drugs designated as essential medicines by the WHO. While this eliminates the problem of the me-toos, it also probably underestimates the overall impact of intellectual property; because cost effectiveness is a criterion for inclusion, very few IP-protected drugs make the essential medicines list. Yet public health systems across the globe must purchase many drugs that are not essential medicines—in part because, as discussed in Chapter 5, patients demand them. If intellectual property leads to rising costs in this broader category and thus mandates the compensatory denial of other services, it *does* present a human rights concern.

Perhaps the essential question, then—and the one about which the least research has been conducted—is how states determine which drugs to buy. I return to this point later, after first addressing a second dimension of drug market failure in Central America.

Fallacy #2: Markets Are Competitive

Critics of intellectual property contend that it introduces monopoly pricing. Yet, in Central America, even without IP, drug markets are often characterized by monopolies. And even where competition does exist, this doesn't always bring down prices. Why?

Some obvious characteristics limit the competitiveness of Central American drug markets. One of these is size: several studies link the number of generic competitors to the size of markets (Hurwitz, Caves, and Harvard Institute of Economic Research, 1986; Scott Morton 2000, 1085–1104). The *number* of generic competitors—not just the existence of a generic option but rather the availability of *multiple* generic options—has been shown to have an impact on the extent to which generic entry prompts a price drop.[7] Yet Central American countries are small to begin with—the entire region boasts a population of around 30 million, fragmented into five national markets—and most consumers and governments are simply too poor to make the market appealing to the largest drug makers. But this is not a "natural" fact; it is the reflection of political decision making on multiple levels. In part, countries like the United States have achieved a flourishing generics industry through the promotion of specific policies, such as the Bolar or "early working" exception that allows generic manufacturers to begin getting their products in the pipeline prior to patent expiry.

Furthermore, specific characteristics of the market, which are heavily shaped by the presence and effectiveness of regulation, make it more or less attractive for generic producers. For example, policies that limit incentives for physicians and pharmacists to dispense higher-cost drugs (by mandating that doctors refer to medications by their generic rather than commercial names on prescriptions, for example, or obligating pharmacists to offer patients generic alternatives when available) also serve to bolster generic competition (Hudson 2000, 205–221) but are not enforced in Central America (ConSuAccion [Consumidores en Acción de Centroamérica] 2007; Kroeger et al. 2001, 605–616).

Lastly, and perhaps most importantly, competitive markets are also constructed through the rigorous monitoring of the drug supply, such that U.S. and European consumers enjoy widespread confidence in the safety of generic alternatives. This is not the case in Central America, where governments lack the capacity and/or political will to insist on tests of bioequivalency and bioavailability, instead typically relying on a company's purported adherence to good manufacturing practices as an indication of its products' quality. As a result, patients frequently express low confidence in the quality of drugs unless they know and trust their brand names, and apparently with good reason: A 2003 study of medications in El Salvador, for example, found that of eighty-seven products sampled, 35 percent were considered inadequate because their content varied more than 10 percent from the composition listed on the label. From samples collected in the Ministry of Health facilities, the proportion found to be inadequate rose to 50 percent (Center for Pharmaceutical Management 2003). This means that fully *half* the drugs provided by the public health system were unsafe for patient consumption. A 2001 study of Mexico and Guatemala found that *no* mechanisms were in place to effectively enforce regulations of the drug supply (Kroeger et al. 2001, 605–616). Although Costa Rica has passed legislation to require bioequivalence testing, it was suspended in 2010 following heavy lobbying from the local generics industry. This has important distorting effects on the tendency of competition to bring down prices. In fact, generics can compete on packaging, dosage, presentation, marketing strategies, and brand reputation, among other factors, and often do in ways that limit the impact of competition on price (Kanavos, Costa-Font, and Seeley 2008, 499–544). While consumers in the United States may purchase generic medicines without consideration for the reputation of the company that produced the drug, the so-called emerging markets, like those of Central America, are dominated by *branded generics*, or products produced by nonoriginator companies but marketed using branding practices. Branded generics have been described as "a half-way house between the patented product and the straight generic product, as they are often promoted by a sales force in a similar fashion to the original" (Moss 2007).

In the Central American context, typically more than 90 percent of the drugs on the market are branded—either originator drugs or branded generics. This leaves less than 10 percent of the market to drugs sold by the name of the active ingredient rather than a distinctive brand name (Martínez and Castro Bonilla 2008; see especially footnote 35). Branded generics typically have higher prices than unbranded generics, and their entry to market is less effective at reducing price because manufacturers work to capture consumer loyalty to specific brands, thus allowing a brand premium to be charged even in the case of nonoriginator drugs. In Central America, manufacturers rely on a host of tactics, including advertising in the mass media, marketing to medical professionals, and kickbacks to pharmacists or doctors who prescribe their product, to ensure brand loyalty (ConSuAccion [Consumidores en Acción de Centroamérica] 2007; Kroeger et al. 2001, 605–616; Martínez and Castro Bonilla 2008). These tactics are used by originator companies *and* the producers of branded generics, whose access to resources may be more limited but whose marketing tool kit remains essentially the same. For this reason, we might consider these producers a sort of "Little Pharma," to use a term coined by Cori Hayden (Hayden 2007).

What's more, these tactics work. A recent study of the Salvadoran pharmaceutical market found that the number of generic competitors was *not* correlated to price, primarily because of brand loyalties: "Despite the existence of competition," Jorge Bogo explains, "The [differences in] prices express the willingness of doctors and patients to pay for the quality differences they perceive among products" (Bogo 2007, 24). Other studies of pharmaceutical pricing in El Salvador would appear to confirm the same thing, showing that consumers pay large markups for generic drugs, which are often priced well in excess of reference prices (Espinoza Fiallos, Marroquín Elías, and Guevara 2009; Espinoza Fiallos and Guevara 2007).

At its most basic level, the argument against pharmaceutical IP rests on the core notion that by delaying the entry of generic drugs to market, IP will limit the competition necessary to reduce prices. But these studies suggest that *even without IP*, in markets like those of Central America, competition often has a limited effect on prices.

To state this differently, it is clear from numerous studies that generic competition is the most effective way to reduce drug prices. Yet it is less clear that we can assume generic competition will occur "naturally" in the absence of intellectual property barriers, particularly in markets like those of Central America—or that this competition, where it occurs, will effectively reduce prices. Is it enough, therefore, to argue against intellectual property because it impedes competition?

This is important, because studies seeking to document the impact of intellectual property on access to medicines frequently compare the existence of low-priced generic drugs on markets without IP protection to their absence in IP-protected markets (Oxfam America 2007; Shaffer and Brenner 2009), but where few if anyone buy a product based on price alone, the existence of a very low priced drug on the market ultimately tells us very little. Furthermore, if patients and physicians lack adequate guarantees that the cheapest drugs on the market are safe for human consumption, what are the ethics of our insistence that access to them, instead of more costly but safer[8] alternatives, is a human right?

These questions return us to the role of the state in shaping market performance (and in being shaped by it). Indeed, this is an essential consideration; ultimately, when taken in isolation, drug prices tell us little. But when examined in context, we may begin to appreciate IP's interaction with other tools and tactics and the way in which this influences human rights outcomes.

State Purchasing

Most of the discussion of IP's impact centers on the availability of drugs on "the market." Yet sometimes this can be deceptive. First of all, the available tools typically give us more information about the private market, yet in poor countries some of the most important and necessary drugs have virtually no presence in private purchasing. For example, the most readily available (though expensive) information about drug purchasing is the databases produced by IMS Health, but these data include only private purchasing, not sales to governments. Similarly, the widely recognized Health Action International (HAI) methodology to measure access to medicines permits important country-to-country comparisons, but because it is based on a survey of drug pricing in pharmacies it tells us little about drugs that private pharmacies simply don't stock. In fact, in relatively small and poor countries like those of Central America, relatively few of the recently developed drugs eligible for intellectual property protection can be found in pharmacies, simply because the costs are prohibitive for patients, who overwhelmingly lack access to insurance and thus must cover pharmacy expenses out of pocket. This means that the most innovative and expensive new medications—those for cancer, HIV/AIDS, and other chronic conditions where intellectual property plays a significant role—are seldom, if ever, purchased directly by patients; the market for these drugs is entirely concentrated in state purchasing.

Across Central America, then, there are two levels of government purchasing. The bulk of the purchasing, in terms of quantity, is comprised of the relatively simple drugs that have, for the most part, been on the market for some time, providing essential treatment for such basic and widespread ailments as infection. Because the states purchase these drugs in large volume, and many local and international generics producers compete for contracts, the per-pill profit margin is low.

By contrast, increasing proportions of state drug expenditures are concentrated in the purchase of specific new drugs to treat small patient populations afflicted with ailments such as cancers, renal insufficiency, transplants, and HIV/AIDS; here, few local producers are able to compete, although distributors for transnational generics companies like Cipla and Ranbaxy have a growing presence in Central America. Although the volume of pills to be purchased is much lower, the prices are stratospherically high; because many of these conditions require sustained treatment for the life of the patient, this segment of the market provides an attractive and sustainable revenue stream for transnational pharmaceutical corporations, both originators and generics. It is here that intellectual property comes into play, and here that such companies resort to a diversity of intertwined tactics, both legal and otherwise, to ensure that their products are the only ones competing for government contracts—and hence to enable them to offer exorbitant prices.

In Guatemala, specific guidelines mandate that the government opt for the most cost effective among a range of options presented during the bidding process, a provision that should ostensibly favor generics, inasmuch as these can be proven safe and effective. In practice, however, the bidding process is often rife with abnormalities, often introduced under the guise of ensuring the safety of the drug supply. The Pan American Health Organization, the office of the Guatemalan human rights ombudsman (known locally as the *Procuraduría de Derechos Humanos*), and the Guatemalan chapter of Transparency International (known locally as *Coalición por la Transparencia*) have all documented anticompetitive irregularities in the bidding processes of 2003 through 2005 (Coalición por la Transparencia 2005; Organización Panamericana de la Salud 2005). These practices amounted to requiring additional documentation from generic bidders attesting to the safety and efficacy of their products, beyond that required in the official bases established for the bidding process, in such a way that it would be prohibitively costly or time consuming for generic bidders to fulfill. As a result, numerous competitions yielded only single bids from originator companies, who were considered to have fulfilled these standards simply by virtue of being originators and granted the contracts.

The story of Abbott's drug Kaletra illustrates how this works. Kaletra, like many of the more recently developed antiretrovirals for the "secondline" treatment of HIV/AIDS, is a multidrug compound composed of two protease inhibitors, lopinavir and ritonavir. In 2005, records from the Guatemalan government's purchase of Kaletra indicated that four companies competed in the open contract bidding process; the contract was awarded to Abbott's representative, J. I. Cohen, at the price of 20.255 quetzales, or roughly US$2.68 at 2005 exchange rates, *per capsule.* The prices offered by competing bidders are not publicly disclosed, but Cipla's distributor, Biocross, S.A., participated in the process, and it seems reasonable to assume their product was offered at a lower price, as they assured me in interviews. It was not selected, presumably due to the aforementioned practices.

In response, generic producers filed writs of amparo[9] to stop the process for Kaletra and other affected drugs, alleging anticompetitive practices. These legal challenges effectively froze the open contracting process until 2008, when the government and industry reached an agreement to continue the open contracting process (Girón 2008). In 2009, the government again announced its intention to purchase Kaletra through the open contract process (Dirección Normativa de Contrataciones y Adquisiciones del Estado). However, because the legal challenges did not eliminate patients' need for treatment, during the three intervening years the Guatemalan government resorted to purchasing Kaletra directly from Abbott. Because the purchases were made outside the open contract system, information about the prices obtained or quantity purchased is not publicly available.

During these years of legal challenges, a new version of Kaletra was introduced, which includes the same active ingredients in a slightly different proportion: Instead of 133 mg of lopinavir and 33 mg of ritonavir per capsule, the new form includes 200 and 50 mg, respectively, and is presented in tablet rather than capsule form. These slight alterations introduce new therapeutic advantages: Patients are required to take fewer pills per day, but, more important, the drug does not require refrigeration, making it one of the very few antiretroviral formulations that are ideally suited to use in many developing countries. Of the drugs recommended by WHO for second-line therapy, this version of Kaletra is the only one available in a heat-stable version.

In 2005, WHO recognized Kaletra as an essential medicine (World Health Organization 2005); since that time, there have been attempts in at least three countries to issue compulsory licenses for this drug.[10] As discussed in Chapter 2, compulsory licensing is a process whereby, in keeping with WTO rules, governments grant permission to a generic manufacturer to produce a lower-cost version of a patented drug when warranted by a national emergency. In these countries, because patents have prevented the introduction of generic Kaletra, compulsory licensing presents a legal and appealing option to reduce prices. In Guatemala, however, as in many less profitable markets, Abbott chose not to patent Kaletra; indeed, a generic version (of the 133/33 concentration) has been on the market since 2000, manufactured by India's Cipla.

In July 2007, mysteriously, the Guatemalan Ministry of Health issued a communiqué adding Kaletra (and AstraZeneca's Nexium) to the list of drugs to which fifteen years of test data protection applied. Because of this retroactive addition of Kaletra to the fifteen-year list, generic versions of the heat-stable version of the drug will not be able to register on the Guatemalan market until November 2015. While Guatemala could choose to issue a compulsory license for this product, compulsory licenses are intended to loosen patents; their applicability to test data has not yet been tested anywhere in the world. In this way, IP is only the latest in a long series of tools used by originator companies to eliminate the competition from the government purchasing process—in this case, for an essential medicine.

The story of AstraZeneca's Nexium, however, is somewhat different. Like Kaletra, Nexium was retroactively included on the list of products enjoying fifteen years of test data protection in 2007; also like Kaletra, generic versions of the drug were already on the market at that time. But unlike Kaletra, Nexium does not represent a significant therapeutic advantage over earlier drugs in its class; as already mentioned, it is often cited as a classic "me-too" (Connolly 2005, A.06-A06; Dyer 2003, 25–25).

Some studies predicting a reduced or insignificant impact of IP argue that governments can, in most cases, shift purchasing away from IP-protected drugs like Nexium to equally effective ones in the same class, thus avoiding paying monopoly prices (Archila et al. 2005; see footnote 8). Theoretically, if Marcia Angell is right, the government could choose to purchase Prilosec instead of Nexium without sacrificing public health. Yet, in Guatemala, the opposite appears to have occurred. After Nexium was introduced, the government shifted its purchasing from omeprazol to esomeprazol, a category in which IP assured that only one bidder would be able to compete for contracts.

These examples illustrate the intersection of IP with state purchasing practices, demonstrating that IP is best conceptualized not as a stand-alone impediment to access but in interaction with other practices and policies. Fundamentally, they underscore three points. First, as the history of Kaletra shows, the mere presence of a generic alternative on the market does not increase access if no one buys it. In Guatemala, a generic version of the 133/33 version of the drug was available for years prior to the introduction of the 200/50 concentration. Yet the state chose to purchase only Abbott's 133/33. Today, thanks to IP, the state purchases only Abbott's 200/50. And while Kaletra remains on the market in generic form, no one is buying it, a fact confirmed by data purchased from IMS Health. The state buys Kaletra from Abbott alone.

Second, the existence of high priced IP protected drugs is not necessarily a human rights concern, when the drugs in question are of dubious therapeutic advantage, like Nexium. Yet their introduction becomes a problem if state purchasing chooses to buy these drugs over cheaper alternatives, as appears to have occurred in Guatemala. Here, IP would appear to contribute needlessly to the unsustainability of state drug budgets. More attention from the health and human rights community is therefore needed to state drug purchasing, and the way in which intellectual property intersects with marketing strategies carried out by industry.

Lastly, more attention is needed to the particularities of IP's implementation in local contexts. However sobering future projections may be, they cannot substitute for the importance of "on the ground" research tracking the application of these laws over time, noting the trajectory of specific drugs and the way health systems have adjusted acquisitions to account for high prices. Judging both by the cases discussed here and by other research on IP since its implementation in Guatemala, it would appear that numerous irregularities have occurred in the application of intellectual property laws in at least that one country (Shaffer and Brenner 2009; Shaffer, Brenner, and Lewis 2009). At minimum, the after-the fact inclusion of Kaletra and Nexium to the fifteen-year list would appear to merit further inquiry; Shaffer and Brenner (2009) also mention attempts to remove other drugs from the market, which would also appear to be based on retroactive applications of the law.

This sort of ongoing monitoring for impact is sorely lacking, and understandably so, given its complexity. Civil society groups are often better positioned than academic researchers to detect changes in national policies and practices governing access to medicines. Yet, in the Central American case, civil society efforts to monitor IP's impact have been limited, in part by a lack of access to reliable information about IP's application from sources other than the affected drug companies themselves.[11] Even for the highly skilled regional public health specialists who participated in the discussions of our CEPIAM network in 2007 through 2009, for example, information about what drugs were denied market access because of IP was extraordinarily hard to come by. Government IP registries typically identified patented molecules by their chemical compounds rather than the name of the commercial product that contains them, thus rendering such lists unintelligible for those without advanced training in biochemistry. Even lists of data-protected drugs, which should inescapably identify a specific commercial product, were seldom readily available, requiring repeat visits to personal contacts at the health ministry. (Here Guatemala was the exception in a positive sense, as such information is posted on government websites.) And the processes by which governments arrived at purchasing decisions—the key site at which IP's impact is felt—were even more inscrutable, so determining the extent to which high prices were affecting state decision making was a tall order indeed.

Despite this, research by network participants produced some intriguing insights. For example, we found not only that many more drugs were off the market because of test data protection in Guatemala—as of December 2009, ninety-eight products enjoyed test data exclusivity in Guatemala, versus only nineteen in El Salvador and five in Nicaragua—but that the specific drugs in question were different. In other words, while one might expect the shorter lists of drugs protected in El Salvador and Nicaragua to be subsets of the longer Guatemalan list, this was not the case. Because test data protection applies to all drugs entering the market, there are various possible reasons for these differences, including drugmakers' decisions where to register and sell their products; differences in the way implementation legislation was drafted, thus narrowing or broadening the scope of test data protection, as already described; or capricious interpretation of existing laws by the health authorities (Godoy and Cerón 2011). Further research is required to understand the functioning of these drug markets and their interactions with IP enforcement bodies.

Conclusion

Ultimately, as the stories of Kaletra and Nexium in Guatemala reveal, the government has spent millions of dollars on originator drugs[12] when generic alternatives did exist. IP holders frequently argue that it is not IP, but rather the inefficiency of state drug delivery systems in poor countries, that impedes access to medicines; in some ways, these findings show that that is partially correct. Yet these findings also reveal that industry's actions contribute to that inefficiency; what's more, its profits thrive under precisely those conditions. In this way, they actually delight in the very circumstances they publicly decry.

Furthermore, defenders of intellectual property point to language in trade agreements insisting on the primacy of public health objectives, and to mechanisms like compulsory licensing in cases of public health emergencies, as evidence that IP constraints can be avoided when health needs warrant flexibility. These findings suggest that such faith is ill founded, for it assumes that IP will interfere with access only in extraordinary cases, in which public policy can step in and solve the problem. In fact, as the Nexium example illustrates, intellectual property is part of the puzzle that raises prices on drugs for gastric reflux. While it is unlikely that gastric reflux would be declared a public health emergency, drugs to treat it are a daily necessity, and their cost can wind up draining public coffers of much-needed resources.

While intellectual property undoubtedly contributes to the creation of monopolies, and hence the prolongation of high drug prices, it does so in conjunction with multiple other factors, including inefficient health systems, aggressive and sometimes illegal marketing practices, and broad, often legitimate fears about drug safety. While this is a complex nexus, for those concerned with health as a human right, it is vitally important to look beyond pricing in expressing concerns about drug access. We need to better understand how states decide which drugs to buy from the range of available options and what these decisions imply in terms of sustainable financing and access to medications. We also need to examine the implications of a failed market in drugs for the poor, to measure access to the drugs that truly matter. Above all, we need to move away from arguments that assume markets alone can provide the answer to drug access problems, and that may unwittingly reinscribe faith in the "free" market when in fact such fallacies have had devastating consequences for public health programs.

Local Politics, Strange Bedfellows, and the Challenges of Human Rights Mobilization

THE DIRECTOR OF ONE OF EL SALVADOR'S best-known pharmaceutical laboratories had his head in his hands. He is proud, he told me, of his family business and of what it contributes to his country's economy: jobs, affordable drugs, opportunities for growth. But he understands that global developments are not pointing in his favor. As a result of the globalization of pharmaceuticals and the onset of intellectual property protection, "hard years are coming for the [Salvadoran] pharmaceutical industry," he said, the discouragement evident in his voice as he rolled up the blueprints he'd shown me for a new plant that might never be built.

At the same time, however, he applauded his government's decision to insert El Salvador deeply and aggressively into the global economy. There's really no other choice, he explained, using the metaphor of a game of chess: When you're in check, you have to move, even if your options are heavily constrained. Although the country's leftist party, the FMLN (Farabundo Martí para la Liberación Nacional), talked about renegotiating global trade deals, electing such a government would be the equivalent of turning over the entire chessboard, sending your pieces crashing to the floor. That's too risky, too frightening for foreign investors, too "disrespectful" of El Salvador's chief commercial partner, the United States.

The dilemmas that the Salvadoran pharmaceutical industry faces are not unique. Across the region, the advent of intellectual property protection represents a fundamental threat to local generic drug manufacturers, who for the most part have enjoyed considerable proximity to political power in past decades. Yet, when faced with pressures from the United States, governments across the region have been unwilling or unable to protect the interests of this homegrown industry, leading to interesting political puzzles for health activists, drug companies, and governments alike. This chapter examines the politics behind these shifting alliances and their implications for access to medicines.

In the campaign against CAFTA's intellectual property provisions, I argue, transnational activists framed the issues in ways that resonated imperfectly with local realities. Based on the experience of other countries, they assumed that local health advocates would oppose IP, that local generics producers would oppose IP, and that these two sectors could form an alliance. Indeed, I made similar assumptions myself when first approaching this work. But in Central America the local health sector was, for the most part, silent on the issue of intellectual property, generics producers were uneven in their opposition, and alliances between the two were fraught with tensions. Over the years, however, I realized that this situation, which I had initially read as a call for "capacity building" on IP in Central America, was in fact the reflection of a mismatch between transnational and local frames for understanding this issue. In this chapter, I explain these disjunctures. I begin with a brief overview of progressive health activism in the region, arguing that a long history of mobilization around the right to health had pitted progressives against the drug industry—local and international—long before the arrival of IP. Against that backdrop, I discuss campaigns against intellectual property in Guatemala, Costa Rica, and El Salvador in detail, arguing that transnational access advocates' framing of the issue fit imperfectly with local politics and priorities. I conclude with some reflections on the implications for future transnational campaigns for trade justice.

Health as a Human Right in Central America: A History of Struggle

As discussed in Chapter 3, Central American countries embraced the idea of health as a human right in the mid-twentieth century and created institutions aimed at delivering on that promise. Yet the resulting health systems reflect and reproduce societal inequalities in many ways. Throughout the 1960s, many Latin American health scholars, particularly those associated with the growing social medicine movement, saw this as misguided and unfair. Advocates in this tradition insisted that poor health should be understood as a reflection of social injustice and that the best way to improve health outcomes was to tackle unjust social arrangements through collective, participatory processes (Tajer 2003, 2023–2027; Waitzkin et al. 2001b, 1592–1601; Waitzkin et al. 2001a, 315–323; Romero, Muñoz, and Vidal 1975, 628–633). Under such an approach, health workers' mission should not be narrowly restricted to biological interventions in response to sickness but much more expansively understood to include work for equity and justice in the distribution of public services. These public services include health care, but also a broader panoply of concerns like the provision of potable water or waste treatment systems. To achieve such changes, rather than a physician-centered model in which experts design biomedical interventions to treat sick individuals, advocates of a model known as primary health care proposed a participatory one in which communities made decisions about their own health needs and priorities and health promoters drawn from these communities themselves spearheaded the task of carrying out initiatives.

Many of these ideas and proposals were reflected in international discussions about primary health care, which reached their apex with the 1978 Declaration of Alma-Ata. This declaration reaffirmed health as a human right and established the global objective of "health for all" by 2000, laying out primary health care as the vehicle through which this would be accomplished; Latin American delegates played leadership roles in crafting it (Villegas de Olazával 2006). As Sandy Smith-Nonini writes, describing the push for primary health care in El Salvador,

> The [primary health care] concept grew out of a consensus among scholars that public health indices reflect not only available health services, but also prevailing socioeconomic conditions—e.g, family income, access to potable water, education, etc. Primary health care's emphasis on prevention and community education was seen as corrective for the biomedical model's myopic curative orientation as an approach to development in Third World nations. (Smith-Nonini 1997, 635)

Indeed, many Central American health professionals played key roles in broader efforts at social change, including the revolutionary movements that gripped the region, in waves of varying intensity, from the 1960s to the 1980s. For these leftist leaders, this vision of health as rooted in community-led transformations for social justice was part of the revolutionary project, a blueprint for a new society. It stood in stark opposition to the technocratic vision of health care as the province of physicians who deployed advanced technology and expert knowledge to combat disease in the bodies of individual patients.

This tension between physician-centered biomedical approaches and community-oriented preventative medicine shaped discussions of health policy in Central America throughout the latter part of the twentieth century. For a time, from the mid-1960s into the 1970s, multilateral health organizations including the Pan American Health Organization (PAHO), the World Health Organization (WHO), and the UN Children's Fund (UNICEF) encouraged Central American governments to adopt the primary health care framework (Palmer 2005, 74; Green 1989, 246–257). Waitzkin and his coauthors credit the leadership of leftist intellectuals such as Salvadoran María Isabel Rodríguez, then at PAHO, with channeling resources and support to the region's governments to underwrite such initiatives (Waitzkin et al. 2001b, 1596). (Significantly, Rodríguez later returned to El Salvador, becoming the first female rector of the University of El Salvador, and today serves as Minister of Health in President Funes's FMLN government; her influence looms large in progressive health circles in El Salvador.)

Yet many critics note that, although Central American governments acceded to the pressures of international agencies during this period, their efforts to implement primary health care were often less than enthusiastic (Green 1989, 246–257; Fiedler 1985, 275; Smith-Nonini 1997, 635–645). Fiedler, for example, suggests that in Guatemala primary health care consisted of little more than a set of limited interventions in the countryside tacked on to otherwise exclusionary structures (Fiedler 1985, 275). Some suggest that the region's governments viewed primary health care's explicit objective of organizing disempowered communities for their own betterment as too threatening to the status quo, at a time when government authorities were struggling to maintain control in the wake of accelerating social protest (Heggenhougen 1984, 217–224; Smith-Nonini 1997, 635–645). This was particularly true in El Salvador and Guatemala, countries that by the late 1970s were teetering on the brink of the massive killing sprees that came to characterize their counterinsurgency wars. But even in peaceful Costa Rica, Morgan argues that party politics and power relations doomed the initiatives implemented briefly in the late 1970s: When rural peasants began to advocate on their own behalf for not only health care, but also for jobs and other measures that ruling elites were not interested in providing, the model was stripped of its participatory character (Morgan 1990, 211–219).

Owing in part to this resistance from local elites, and in part to shifting political winds within international institutions, state health programs rooted in the perspective of social medicine fell out of favor in the 1980s. As Morgan explains,

> Responding to the unstable world economic climate in 1980–81 and government reports of dissatisfaction with community participation, WHO and UNICEF quietly shifted their priorities from community participation to other areas. The rhetoric of participation continued to be important, for a time, but in practical terms the initiative had declined by 1982. (Morgan 1990, 218)

In the 1980s and 1990s, Latin American health systems were restructured along the lines of macroeconomic policies favored by the World Bank, ostensibly to improve equity and efficiency (Tajer 2003, 2023–2027). As one study sums up this wave of changes, "In almost all countries of [Latin America], the health reforms included three basic policies: decentralization of services, downsizing of the public sector through privatization and outsourcing, and the offering of minimum health service packages to the indigent populations at no cost" (Homedes, Ugalde, and Rovira Forns 2005, 691). In Central America, particularly in El Salvador and Guatemala, many of these changes were introduced in the context of postwar assistance when support from the international community reshaped spending priorities in significant ways. The broad emphasis on bottom-up participation shaping holistic and preventative approaches to community health was abandoned in favor of vertical interventions targeting specific diseases (Donahue 1989, 258–269) or minimum coverage levels for the poorest (Morales 2004, 7). Similarly, health systems were decentralized, a move justified by the need to spread access to care beyond urban areas. In Guatemala, for example, the Inter-American Development Bank funded a program called the Integrated System for Health Attention/ Coverage Extension, which brought medical services to some areas for the first time. But it was criticized for contracting out essential services to NGOs ill positioned to encourage participation (Maupin 2009, 1456–1463) and lacking sufficient funds to deliver quality comprehensive care (Morales 2004, 7).

In the wake of these reforms, catchwords like *primary health care* still pepper state programs, but contemporary initiatives are carried out in fundamentally different ways than those advocated by social medicine specialists. For example, in 1990s El Salvador, the Ministry of Health undertook efforts to bring health care to rural areas previously controlled by the FMLN guerrillas. Although the government's initiatives were ostensibly conducted to promote citizen participation, they were often broadly rejected by the communities they were intended to benefit. These communities, who had participated in popular health efforts spearheaded by the FMLN or Catholic Church a decade before, embraced a different, more bottom-up understanding of the role of nonphysicians in promoting improved health. As Smith-Nonini explains, "Confrontations grew out of a reverberating dialectic between the Ministry's commitment to an extremely centralized, biomedical model dominated by physicians and the popular system's commitment to health care delivery with a strong degree of community control that is based on local lay health promoters" (1997, 638). In this context, the need for highly trained personnel to supervise the use of medicines was one of the government's justifications for its physician-centric model (Smith-Nonini 1997, 635–645); while popular approaches did not challenge the importance of access to medicine, discussions about health that began with medicines were often seen as fatally rooted in the curative biomedical model.

These contending perspectives continue to dominate discussions about health today. As Smith-Nonini elaborates, "The end of the war signified more a truce than a real political reconciliation in El Salvador. . . . In the meantime, the two sides still see each other as enemies (now in the political arena rather than the battlefield) and continue to skirmish over control over all forms of social capital, including the moral legitimacy that attaches to health care" (Smith-Nonini 1997,.642). The flashpoints of tension are familiar: community participation, preventative medicine, the use of health promoters. For example, a 2002 study of the Basic Systems of Integral Health in El Salvador published by one of the networks of progressive health advocates concluded,

> In practice, this unilateral, unconsulted proposal lacks real citizen participation. The Ministry of Health should make real efforts to open these structures and make the principles enunciated in the documents coherent, since the strategy of primary health care is based on the participation of an organized community, in which the communities themselves define the axes and priorities for the health system. (Marroquín Elías 2003, 4)

In other countries of the region, political polarization is less pronounced than in El Salvador, and as a result the confrontation over approaches to health may not be as direct. Yet the same questions of where health interventions should focus their energies reverberate through contemporary discussions. While intellectual property critics express concerns over IP's impact on the region's poorest residents, many progressive health activists continue to see access to medicines—especially to the most recently developed medicines, rather than basic antidiarrheals and others that have been off-patent for many years—as important, but dangerously linked to the prevailing assumption that technological fixes can be found to solve health problems fundamentally rooted in social injustice. To address the root causes, they argue, we should focus on things like access to food and water, as a way to prevent people from getting sick in the first place.

Strange Bedfellows: The Politics of Intellectual Property

When CAFTA brought concerns about intellectual property and access to medicine to the fore in 2004, it posed challenges for progressive health activists, who until that time had been primarily engaged in national struggles over ensuring quality and equity in state health services. But the frame of transnational trade politics also created opportunities.

Across Central America, and in the United States, CAFTA's negotiation and ratification touched off a vibrant series of protests. Activists organized fora and marches, conducted media campaigns, lobbied elected officials, and engaged in civil disobedience. New transnational coalitions emerged, with a number of differently situated participants. The most salient of these, based in the United States but established in partnership with Central American organizations, was the Stop CAFTA Coalition. Participants in this coalition hailed from a diverse list of organizations of at least four types. These included, first of all, groups first formed during the civil wars of the 1980s, like the Committee in Solidarity with the People of El Salvador (CISPES), as well as faith-based groups, such as the Maryknoll Office for Global Concerns, who had been active in Central America throughout the wars. Although many activists in these groups had remained committed to their cause over the years, the salience of Central American issues in U.S. politics had faded; CAFTA revived interest, albeit temporarily, in this world region and revitalized solidarity groups whose influence had waned. The groups, while typically lacking sizable financial resources, offered historic connections to specific Central American countries and communities and a small but highly motivated membership base that was reenergized by participation in the anti-CAFTA campaign. Second, large transnational humanitarian groups like Oxfam and Doctors Without Borders joined in these efforts, bringing significant resources, both financial and reputational. Third, in Central America, although there were efforts to build coalitions in opposition to CAFTA, the grassroots organizations active in these coalitions were, for the most part, issue specific: indigenous rights groups in Guatemala, vendors of pirated CDs in El Salvador, peasant organizations, unions, and environmentalists. And lastly, the inclusion of IP brought a novel sector to the table: In some countries, representatives of local generic drug companies participated in the lobbying effort against CAFTA.

Yet, among the issues involved in CAFTA, intellectual property received very little attention relative to concerns about agricultural sustainability, labor rights, or the environment. While these latter issues drew on the concerns and expertise of long-established civil society groups in Central America, IP was a relative newcomer. Not only were few organizations equipped to understand its implications in detail—a formidable challenge, given the general inscrutability of CAFTA's IP chapter—but also, IP intersected only peripherally with the central concerns of longstanding health rights advocates in the region. As a result, in Central America the health sector did not participate in any organized fashion in debates over CAFTA. Although in South America a group of ten ministers of health jointly signed a declaration in May 2006 expressing their opposition to new intellectual property norms, in Central America no ministers of health took public stands to this effect. Doctors' associations were similarly silent.

During the campaign, therefore, most of the general information about intellectual property was provided by the transnational humanitarian groups (especially Oxfam and Doctors Without Borders), with country-specific context filled in by local generics producers in some countries. While grassroots advocacy groups embraced transnational analyses and used them to mobilize in the context of agreement contestation, they did not develop an intellectual property focus of their own.

In the end, legislatures across the region ratified the agreement despite mass protests. In El Salvador, anti-CAFTA activists occupied the legislative chambers in an effort to forestall the vote on December 16, 2004; security flushed them out, and legislators, locked inside overnight, brought CAFTA to the floor at 3 am. As Rose Spalding writes, "In an overnight process that truncated public hearings, violated institutional procedures, and precluded meaningful legislative debate, El Salvador became the first country to ratify CAFTA" (2007, 117). In Guatemala, on March 8, 2005, with thousands of protestors converging on Congress, deputies moved to hastily approve the agreement without subjecting it to the standard procedure of three readings normally required for the ratification of international treaties. In Costa Rica, a country with deeper democratic traditions, the agreement was put to a popular referendum in October 2007; after months of unprecedented mobilization on both sides, it passed by a narrow margin amid allegations of illegal campaigning by the U.S. ambassador.

In the following pages, I explore resistance against the agreement in each country in more depth.

Guatemala

Guatemala was the only Central American country where this issue achieved broad public attention and media coverage and furthermore the country whose situation as a result of CAFTA attracted the most attention internationally. This is no coincidence: As the largest economy and the most populous nation in Central America, Guatemala is also home to the offices of FEDEFARMA (Federación Centroamericano de Laboratorios Farmacéuticos), the originator companies' lobbying organization for the region as a whole, and, since the arrival of IP, Guatemala has been the country in which the largest number of pharmaceutical patents have been granted and data exclusivity applied most rigorously (Godoy and Cerón 2011, 1186). The country's position as a regional leader undoubtedly also influenced Doctors Without Borders' decision to establish its Central American local office there. So when CAFTA came along, Guatemala served as the Central American headquarters for transnational organizations on both sides of the issue, and Guatemalan health politics provided the main ring in which they sparred.

Guatemala was also the only Central American country that saw the formation of a coalition of organizations working specifically on intellectual property issues, the Alianza Civil por el Acceso a Medicamentos (ACAM), which began in 2003. The group enjoyed diverse participation from HIV/AIDS patients, public health advocates, unions in the health sector, and other groups, and it benefited from the expertise, energy, and material resources contributed by Doctors Without Borders. It carried out activities ranging from lobbying Congress, participating in fora, and disseminating information through publications. While short lived, it played a role in driving changes in Guatemala's intellectual property policies during 2003 through 2005.

As discussed in Chapter 3, for a period of several years prior to CAFTA's passage, the country's IP legislation veered dramatically back and forth: As Table 4.1 shows, the country went from having no test data protection, to having protection for fifteen years (Congreso de la República de Guatemala 2000), to having no protection again (Congreso de la República de Guatemala 2003a), to having five years of protection (Congreso de la República de Guatemala 2003b), to again having no protection (Congreso de la República de Guatemala 2004), and finally to reestablishing the five-year period (Congreso de la República de Guatemala 2005).

According to at least one participant in the effort, the involvement of transnational groups—not only Doctors Without Borders but also the peer organizations with whom they communicated, including Oxfam, Health GAP, and many other public health and human rights advocates based in

TABLE 4.1 Changing test data protection in Guatemala.

Date	Law	Number of years of protection
August 31, 2000	Decreto 57-2000	15 years
January 28, 2003	Decreto 76-2002, published as Acuerdo 6-2003	0 years
April 15, 2003	Decreto 9-2003	5 years
November 19, 2004	Decreto 34-2004	0 years
March 18, 2005	Decreto 30-2005	5 years

the United States and Europe—gave local activists an important boost (Miranda n.d.). These dynamics were also evident when I observed ACAM activities in 2004. For Miranda, the participation of powerful transnational actors helped elevate the issue from something of only limited interest to a broad, public issue, of which many Guatemalan citizens became aware. In this sense, the opening afforded by the trade agreement was a boon for Guatemalan activism: Were it not for CAFTA, these transnational groups would not have been interested in local politics, and, had they not been invested in driving change there, most likely little would have taken place to revert the aggressive intellectual property laws already passed.

In many ways, ACAM's accomplishment was striking. After all, the group was successful—temporarily—at reversing a law that was vocally supported by powerful transnational companies, the U.S. government, and their supporters in Guatemala, including the American Chamber of Commerce, FEDEFARMA, and other private industry groups. ACAM's efforts also undoubtedly contributed to the inclusion of some "opportunities" for public health in Guatemalan IP law, as shown in Table 3.2 in Chapter 3. For an intense few months, a group of ragtag activists had knocked transnational capital on its heels.

A March 2005 diplomatic cable recently published by Wikileaks sheds some light on this period as seen from the perspective of U.S. Ambassador John Hamilton. According to Hamilton, securing increased protection for pharmaceutical IP had "consumed in aggregate more of our full-time attention than any other issue in recent months" (Hamilton 2011). Hamilton reported that the issue had been gravely misunderstood by Guatemalan government officials, who, on discovering that the social security institute paid exorbitantly high prices for medicines, assumed that PhRMA companies were conspiring with hospital higher-ups to bilk the public of millions. Thanks to the work of Doctors Without Borders (which the cable reports "coached" local NGOs and ASINFARGUA [Asociación de Industriales Farmacéuticos Guatemaltecos], the generics lobby) and political figures associated with the generics industry, the general public accepted the basic premise of the opposition's argument. The U.S. embassy, in response, was forced to unleash what Hamilton describes as a "public diplomacy blitzkrieg" to ensure passage of the bill reinstating data exclusivity. This involved, among other things, repeated threats that the entire trade deal would founder if Guatemala did not reinstate data protection: Hamilton himself published an editorial in one of the largest circulation dailies warning that if Guatemala failed to "take its obligations seriously," the entire trade deal hung in the balance (Hamilton 2005). Similarly, a series of visits by a delegation of U.S. congressional staffers and by a former U.S. ambassador emphasized that, as Hamilton wrote, "CAFTA would likely die on the vine without immediate action on data protection" (Hamilton 2011).

The cable is instructive, not least because it makes evident what many long suspected, in terms of the high-pressure lobbying for intellectual property undertaken by the U.S. government, largely behind closed doors. It also provides a frank description of the Embassy's strategy on the matter, concluding:

> A lesson learned on making the IPR case: The core argument against IPR for drugs pits transnationals' profits against the poor and infirm. It is simple and effective, and we found no magic bullets for refuting it. The information we tend to push back is so complex that listeners quickly tune out. We were more effective with a Socratic approach, engaging the critics before an audience and asking them to explain their concerns in detail. How, exactly, will data protection make generics unavailable in poor countries? What drugs that are critical to public health are kept out of poor countries by data protection? Without exception, they slipped up when challenged to explain how data protection works and affects access to generics. The most common assertion was that data protection adds five years to the life of a

patent. Whenever we could say, "No it doesn't," the audience was interested in learning why not. It is time consuming, but it erodes the credibility of the sound bites that otherwise resonate so well. (Hamilton 2011)

"The sound bites that resonate so well," of course, are the attempts by access advocates to formulate compelling causal arguments to motivate political action: Passing CAFTA will take essential drugs off the market, to put it one way, or will generate—in *The New York Times*'s terms—a "body count" of X number. Yet, as Hamilton's memo describes, and as I saw in action across Central America, such arguments suffered a sort of technocratic death by a thousand cuts. Although they are not essentially false—intellectual property does pit life against profits—the technical mechanisms by which IP's adoption has an impact on health are infinitely complex, and it takes deep knowledge of IP law to sustain the argument through all its twists and turns.

In the Central American context, most activists never acquired this deep knowledge, relying instead on the transnational organizations to formulate arguments against intellectual property. In my interviews with many grassroots activists, they seemed genuinely concerned, yet not deeply informed about the ins and outs of IP law; the perception mentioned in the cable, that data protection would tack on additional years to a patent's life, was widespread, yet none of my local activist informants could point to the place in the law from which it derived. In this context, local expertise sometimes wore thin and was exposed, as the embassy notes. As Vargas Ayala reports, the generic industry stood in for consumer participation in discussions of these issues, and the health sector was largely absent; to make matters worse, the Ministry of Health flip-flopped on the issue, supporting both laws repealing data exclusivity and laws reinstating it (Vargas Ayala 2006).

Although ACAM's mobilization was successful in reverting some of the most aggressive intellectual property legislation in the world, these victories were ultimately short lived. In part, this was because the effort focused on the trade agreement's negotiation and ratification rather than its implementation. Once the ratification battle was lost, the more powerful transnational organizations turned their attention to other trade battles emerging in the Andean region. This turning-away of transnational attention was felt particularly acutely after CAFTA because the period co-incided with Doctors Without Borders' departure from the country, for reasons unrelated to CAFTA itself. While the smaller grassroots groups remained concerned about this issue, without the active accompaniment and resources of transnational allies they lacked the capacity to track or influence implementation. And for the generics industry, other avenues may have proved more attractive for advancing their interests: ASINFARGUA's director, Luis Velásquez, accepted a position in the executive branch of government; after that, he told me in 2009 that all the concerns he had raised in previous years were now resolved. Remarkably, at the time of our last meeting he simultaneously held positions as director of ASINFARGUA and private secretary to the president.

Ultimately, this meant that Guatemala was left without an on-the-ground advocate for access-friendly interpretations of intellectual property during the implementation phase. As a result, laws were drafted with virtually no public scrutiny; the widespread perception was that since CAFTA had passed, few (if any) options remained. Indeed, CAFTA's passage mandated many changes; but others, such as the indefinite granting of patent extensions or the application of test data protection to the widest possible set of products, were imposed despite being unnecessary under the terms of the agreement, as discussed in Chapters 2 and 3.

Costa Rica

In Costa Rica, by contrast, there was massive mobilization against CAFTA as a whole but considerably less around the issues of medicines and intellectual property, a somewhat surprising outcome given the recognized importance of Costa Rica's health system. As in Guatemala, the health sector sat largely on the sidelines in the debate over the trade agreement, grassroots groups mobilized but lacked deep knowledge, and the generics industry stepped into the breach.

Most of the work on IP was led by Román Macaya, president of the Costa Rican national association of agrochemical producers. Because CAFTA applied the same provisions to agrochemicals as to pharmaceuticals—indeed, agrochemicals were granted a monopoly term twice as long—he and other agrochemical manufacturers opposed the agreement for their own reasons. A biochemist with a PhD from UCLA and an MBA from

Wharton, Macaya is a member of a family who own Rimacsa, a generic agrochemicals company, though in his public advocacy about CAFTA he focused on its impact on access to medicines, a topic about which he was very knowledgeable. He had dedicated considerable energy to research in Costa Rica's patent office, trying to dig up information about which drugs were already patented and which requests were coming in. On the basis of this and other research, he gave frequent public presentations to Costa Rican and international audiences alike, on the dangers of CAFTA's intellectual property provisions.

Macaya was in many ways an impressive interlocutor: Well informed and savvy, he switched effortlessly between English and Spanish and dipped into data-heavy slides explaining highly technical provisions of law as smoothly as he did into reflections on development and national sovereignty. Yet he was far from an activist firebrand: Indeed, many anti-CAFTA activists privately expressed some skepticism about his embrace of human rights. As Hayden writes about the expansion of generics chain Farmacias Similares in Mexico, "[This] is indisputably a businessman's revolution, executed by an enterprise laying claim to a social-nationalist (not to be confused with socialist) conscience" (2007, 486). Indeed, the evocative phrase Mexican generic pharmaceuticals magnate Víctor González Torres used to describe himself —"Che Guevara in a Mercedes" (Hayden 2007, 486)—captures something of the figure Macaya cut in these discussions.

And by and large, for better or worse, Macaya was acting alone, a fact he himself recognized and lamented when I met with him in 2007. While many grassroots anti-CAFTA activists were concerned about this issue, few had enough command of the technicalities to speak publicly on it in any depth.

Albin Chaves, director of pharmacotherapy at Costa Rica's Social Security Institute and the person in charge of purchasing drugs for all state facilities, was also largely silent on the issue. Chaves collaborated with a study conducted by the Ministry of External Trade (COMEX) that was frequently mentioned in the discussions about intellectual property in Costa Rica. The study, which was never published in its entirety, analyzed a single year—2003—as an illustration and determined that at that time, of the list of drugs registered in the country, there were only seven that had been registered in the last five years. If test data exclusivity had been in effect then, only originator versions of those seven substances would have been available at the time. However, for all seven, the Caja had purchased originator versions anyway; in large part this was due to the limited competitiveness of certain niches of the Costa Rican pharmaceuticals market and the resultant lack of generic competitors (on this point, see Chapter 2). Therefore, the study concluded, the introduction of intellectual property would not fundamentally have changed the outcome at all.

When I spoke with both Chaves and Federico Valerio, the lead IP negotiator for the Costa Rican government, about this study, both acknowledged that if it were replicated in a different year, the findings could be different.[1] In this sense, neither insisted that intellectual property would *never* have an impact on the Caja's ability to purchase generics, only that in the immediate short run only a minimal impact was anticipated. This echoed the strategy used by CAFTA promoters in Guatemala and described in the leaked cable: No one denied that the agreement contained a raft of provisions that could produce monopolies, arguing instead on highly technical grounds that its impact could be contained with responsible policy making. While intellectual property opponents warned in dire terms about the collapse of health systems, IP advocates or apologists trotted out single-digit lists of drugs and ticked off the reasons why each one was not a concern. The net result of this highly technical level of discussion was that, when transnational groups like Oxfam, Doctors Without Borders, and HealthGAP looked for someone to speak to the impact of the agreement on access to medicines in the region's only truly effective public health system, the most viable candidate was Román Macaya (Health GAP 2005; Goodman 2007).

Many of my interviewees told me that the Costa Rican health sector's silence on this issue was a reflection of politics: As a political appointee, Chaves enjoyed limited liberties to criticize a trade agreement that the executive branch clearly supported, and generic producers' financial interests lay in preserving their positive relationship with the Caja, leading them to stay out of politics. These are certainly plausible explanations. But Chaves himself offered a different answer. From where he sat as the man in charge of negotiating drug prices with transnational producers, he told me, it was in his interest to maintain positive relationships with drugmakers like Merck and Novartis. As important as he believed it was to ensure that Costa Rican legislation preserved the possibility of issuing a compulsory license, for example, it only made sense to contemplate the use of such tactics as a last resort if friendly negotiations for lower prices broke down. While transnational activists wanted Costa Rica to use compulsory licensing, Chaves insisted that such actions might perhaps lead to lower prices on a single drug in isolation, but what about all the other products he needed to source from the same supplier? If larger countries faced retaliation from drugmakers when they sought compulsory licenses, surely the options for tiny Costa Rica were more constrained still. In that context, Chaves said, taking bold positions against the industry might win him supporters among certain international organizations, but it could ultimately limit his ability to do right by his patients.

El Salvador

In El Salvador, similarly, despite a long history of activism and particularly notable participation in massive organizing around the right to health in recent years, the health sector was largely silent on the issue of intellectual property and its likely impact. In my interviews with leading members of progressive health networks, including the Asociación Salvadoreña Promotora de Salud, Asociación de Promotores y Promotoras Comunales Salvadoreños, Centro para la Defensa del Consumidor, health workers' unions, and Fundación Maquilishuat, local health advocates emphasized their ongoing concerns about privatization of the health system, the quality (or lack thereof) of publicly available health services, and the commercialization of health more broadly. They were very receptive to arguments that trade agreements prioritized the interests of transnational capital over public health and indeed were uniformly opposed to the agreement. But ultimately, they were reluctant to involve themselves in a movement that consisted entirely of advancing access to markets for generic drugs.

Similarly, in my interviews with executives at the most prominent generic laboratories, including Laboratorios Ancalmo, López, Teramed, Vijosa, and others, all expressed a deep-seated suspicion of the popular health movements that had dominated recent discussions of health policy. While those affiliated with smaller companies were less aware of the finer points of intellectual property and its implications, those at the helm of more prominent businesses minced no words in explaining how

CAFTA would have a negative impact on their industry. Some, like José Mario Ancalmo of Laboratorios Ancalmo, were extremely knowledgeable; Ancalmo serves not only as president of the Salvadoran generic pharmaceutical industry association, INQUIFAR (Asociación de Industriales Químico-Farmacéuticos de El Salvador), but as vice president of the Latin America–wide generic association ALIFAR (Asociación Latinoamericana de Industrias Farmacéuticas) and holds a doctorate in intellectual property from the University of Buenos Aires, where he studied under renowned intellectual property critic Carlos Correa. He described the trade agreement as clearly a vehicle through which U.S. pharmaceutical companies were seeking to expand their control of the market and elaborated a list of ways it would be prejudicial to competition in El Salvador. But when asked if, for those very reasons, he supported the Salvadoran organizations of the left that opposed the agreement, he balked.

There are many historical reasons for this mutual mistrust. First, progressive health activists and generic drug producers were on opposite sides of their country's armed conflict from 1980 to 1992, an ideological and political difference that continues to reverberate today. Among health activists, all of my interviewees attributed their involvement in activism to the experience of the war; even activists who entered adulthood after the war's end began their personal stories with the history of the conflict and unequivocally traced their sympathies to the FMLN. When discussing their view of health reforms, they identified the generics industry as part of the oligarchy who opposed them throughout the war. Indeed, the families of at least two former right-wing presidents, Alfredo Cristiani and Tony Saca, own some of the industry's leading firms; Miguel Lacayo, minister of the economy during the CAFTA negotiations process, heads another.

Generics producers, in turn, echoed these sentiments from the other side. While leaders like José Mario Ancalmo were very familiar with the ways CAFTA would disadvantage their industry, they were reluctant to oppose the agreement publicly and indeed issued public statements indicating tepid support for the agreement while expressing concerns in private. Industry leaders accused health activists of making the question of contemporary medicines policy a symbolic site onto which to project historical animosities and rile up class hatred. As one executive told me, when I asked him why he rejected the idea of a strategic alliance for access to medicines, the differences were irreconcilable. "There are two ways to think about humankind," he explained, "and we're always going to be at permanent war." He proceeded to describe a Marxist worldview in which conflict served as the engine of history—the view he said Salvadoran leftists embraced—and a capitalist one in which cooperation led to progress, which was his own view. "The problem is that it's harder for us to sell responsibility than it is for them to sell resentment."

In a small country, these broad ideological disagreements also become personal. For example, many pharmaceutical executives mentioned Eduardo Espinoza, a leading figure in the progressive health movement and among the industry's most fervent critics, citing his personal background during the war as a reason it was impossible to work with the left. Espinoza is a former FMLN collaborator who became a prisoner of war and was subsequently released in a high-profile prisoner exchange when the guerrillas captured the president's daughter (Hernández 2010); as of this writing, he serves as vice minister of health in the FMLN government of Mauricio Funes. And if the pharmaceutical executives speak of him in less than generous terms, the feeling is mutual; on national television in a July 6, 2010, debate about drug pricing, he called the generics industry "terrorists" for holding the public's health hostage to their inflated price schemes, saying they made more money than narcotraffickers; when asked about the statement subsequently, he reaffirmed it.

Second, these ideological differences have translated into a history of concrete differences on specific points of substance. The private sector umbrella organization ANEP (Asociación Nacional de la Empresa Privada), with which INQUIFAR is affiliated, was among the most vocal supporters of the health reforms of the late 1990s and early 2000s, which spurred the massive protest movements that for many define the period (Lemus and Baires Quezada 2011). Beginning in 1998, a coalition calling itself the Tripartite Commission formed to oppose the proposed reforms. This commission was composed of doctors' unions in the social security institute and public health systems and the physicians' professional association, the Colegio de Médicos. The health workers conducted a strike from November 1999 to March 2000, protesting a World Bank- and IDB (Inter-American Development Bank) -funded initiative to partially privatize the health system; during this time, dozens of public marches were held, some drawing as many as 50,000 participants in support of the health workers (Almeida 2010, 319). These efforts were successful in forcing an end to the proposed restructuring and laying the groundwork for even more massive mobilizations in reaction to another effort at partial privatization several years later.

In 2002, with the support of the private sector, the executive branch introduced a series of proposed reforms that again included a partial privatization scheme. From September 2002 to June 2003, health unions went on strike again, calling on their organized allies in other civil society movements to support them. The result was a series of highway blockades, marches, and manifestations, some drawing as many as 200,000 participants (Almeida 2010, 327). Among the most memorable of these were the so-called white marches, in which thousands of health workers took to the streets wearing their white lab coats. Again, this movement successfully stymied efforts to privatize the public health system in El Salvador. Some view it as among the most important strikes in the history of El Salvador (Almeida 2010, 319), and it was certainly a watershed moment for contemporary organizing around health rights (Smith-Nonini 2010).

For many years prior to the arrival of CAFTA, drug prices had been broadly perceived as a priority issue. Beginning in 2002, a coalition of progressive health groups called the Red APSAL (Acción para la Salud en El Salvador) drafted a bill to reform the industry (Lemus and Baires Quezada 2011). Among other things, the bill proposed the creation of price and quality controls to reduce the cost of all medicines and ensure their effectiveness. The FMLN later proposed a similar but competing bill. Both were fiercely opposed by the generics industry and foundered with the larger health sector reforms. The generics industry, on the other hand, has proposed to reduce prices by eliminating the sales tax on medicines or instituting preferences in state purchasing practices to favor local producers (Espinoza Fiallos, Marroquín Elías, and Guevara 2009).

In recent years, a number of studies have documented high prices in the Salvadoran pharmaceutical market across the board, including the products of both generic and originator companies. Strikingly, multiple studies found Salvadoran generic drugs to be priced, on average, nearly *thirty times* the international reference prices (ConSuAccion [Consumidores en Acción de Centroamérica] 2007; Espinoza Fiallos, Marroquin

Elias, and Guevara 2009; Espinoza Fiallos and Guevara 2007; Consejo Centroamericano de Protección al Consumidor, CONCADECO 2008).

On some products for which international comparison prices are available through Health Action International's databases, El Salvador's prices were found to be the highest in the world (Espinoza Fiallos and Guevara 2007). As of this writing, progressive health activists were working under the leadership of Eduardo Espinoza to pass a bill to fundamentally restructure the pharmaceuticals market through the introduction of price and quality controls, among other mechanisms. The generics industry continues to oppose such initiatives.

If the Salvadoran case is extreme in its polarization, it is not unique. Across Central America, transnational campaigns' calls to defend access to access to generics in the CAFTA period sat awkwardly with longstanding political divisions. And stakes are high in Central American politics, in a way that can be easy to forget from the comfortable remove of the North. In 2005, Guatemalan journalist Marielos Monzón and a colleague received death threats that some attributed to their advocacy on this issue (Vargas Ayala 2006); in El Salvador, during her involvement in the 1999 struggle against privatization, health activist Margarita Posada was kidnapped, held for two days, and warned to "stop talking," a threat she interpreted as retaliation for her efforts (Lemus and Baires Quezada 2011). My point here is not to invite speculation about the origins of such incidents or to suggest these women are the only victims of politically motivated violence in postwar Central America; rather, I aim to emphasize that in contexts where people continue to pay with their lives for their politics, questions of trust weigh heavily in the formation of political alliances. This makes it extraordinarily difficult to imagine setting aside decades-old differences to advance a common platform when interests align on a single issue like IP.

Lastly, Central American health activists may also have reacted with some skepticism to the way the issue was framed by transnational groups for another reason. As discussed at the outset of this chapter, many Central American health activists questioned the primacy of what they refer to as "curative" medicine, based on the model of biomedical interventions in the individual patient body rather than collective processes to address the social determinants of health. In this context, while access to medicines is undeniably important, it tends to be viewed as a limited and late entry point for a rights-based approach to health; particularly in poor countries like these, access to uncontaminated water or restrictions on pesticide exposure for agricultural workers might be seen as more desirable "upstream" interventions in the interests of entire communities.

There are important disjunctures, then, in the ways transnational and local human rights activists approach this issue. These include perceptions about potential campaign partners, but they go deeper than that; while everyone is concerned about lack of access to medicines, the way the problem is framed in Geneva sometimes resonates poorly with the way it's seen from San Salvador.

Reflections on Transnational Human Rights Advocacy in the Era of "Free" Trade

Of course, if transnational access to medicines advocates miss some of the finer points of Central American health politics, perhaps we ought to cut them some slack. As Peter Drahos reminds us (Drahos 2007, 11), the struggle against IP maximalism must simultaneously be fought on many shifting fronts, and, although organizations like Oxfam or Doctors Without Borders may seem flush with cash compared to grassroots groups in Central America, their resources pale in comparison to those of their adversaries in industry and government. It's a bit of a tall order, then, to ask them to maintain sustained, supportive, simultaneous relationships with differently situated movements for health in every corner of the world.

And, similarly, the fact that this issue looks differently when seen through the complex prism of local political alliances is ultimately unsurprising; no one would argue that Geneva and Guatemala City are gripped by the same political forces. My point, therefore, is not simply to note these empirical observations about IP politics in Central America, nor to pillory the efforts of transnational advocacy groups without whose work the picture would be grimmer still. Rather, I am interested in asking what the implications of these findings are for the way we think about human rights today. As more and more human rights campaigning shifts to the terrain of social and economic rights, and more and more social policy is shaped by international commercial law, I believe there are important lessons we can discern from this experience.

First, as this case study illustrates, significant disjunctures can occur between the way issues are perceived by long-term participants in local rights struggles and the way they are framed transnationally. In the cases examined here, although Central American activists seized the opportunity to collaborate with better-resourced transnational groups when the CAFTA context made this possible, the framing of the problem and the selection of protagonists projected transnational political priorities onto the Central American context. On one level, my point here is to show why this didn't work (or only worked in a very limited way). Given varying levels of access to resources, the passing of the transnational gaze across the territory of small and—in global terms—geopolitically insignificant countries like those of Central America creates, in and of itself, a political opportunity structure. Sometimes that can be used to drive substantive change, as it did in Guatemala during the period when Doctors Without Borders led the ACAM coalition's work. Yet the transnational gaze is always fleeting. Ultimately, unless local activists take up an issue, any gains made during the period of the transnational campaigning may be short lived.

In the case of Central American IP campaigning, there was very little local uptake of the issue because key elements of the campaign did not resonate with leading local actors. Progressive health advocates had limited awareness of intellectual property issues, because their priorities were focused on a vision of medicine and health in which access to the latest high-tech drugs was not a primary concern. Local generics producers backed the campaign, but in unpredictable ways; as prominent members of their countries' industrial elites, they were politically aligned with forces who supported the trade agreement, and over time their proximity to state power opened other avenues for defending their interests that were more palatable to them than protest. An alliance between generics producers and progressive health advocates was politically unsustainable. Ultimately, therefore, the limited gains made possible by transnational attention during the ratification struggle did not translate into long-term benefit for Central Americans. Implementation took place largely without critical attention to the issue, as transnational efforts were now focused elsewhere and local actors turned to other tactics to advance their objectives. One obvious conclusion, therefore, is that, simply to ensure the sustainability of trade justice efforts, we should look to ensure greater alignment between transnational and local priorities in future struggles.

Second, as we contemplate future transnational campaigns, we need to think more critically about how power imbues various positions in advocacy networks. In an earlier era of human rights campaigning, when most transnational advocacy work focused on civil and political rights, much of the work focused on specific country contexts; the early days of Amnesty International, for example, saw campaigns centered on freeing individual prisoners adopted by Amnesty groups in the North, and thus responding to specific information generated "on the ground" in the country in question.

The transition toward greater inclusion of social and economic rights, however, has led to a greater focus on the role of transnational corporations and economic structures and with it a greater frequency of issue-based campaigning that cuts across country contexts. On the one hand, this is very much a good thing, offering a potent response to earlier critiques that human rights groups portrayed abuses as stemming from the savagery of Third World leaders rather than the international systems that put them in power (Mutua 2002). On the other hand, however, this shift creates new challenges for global advocacy groups: Oftentimes, they may be selecting a theme for campaigning and then, by necessity, identifying allies in each concrete context. This is an inherently top-down approach. Beyond the question of what works, then, lies a deeper query: In a world full of so many injustices, who's to say which battles we pick in the name of human rights? Who decides?

Theoretical approaches to transnational activist activity tend to assume that conflicts become "verticalized" when they receive international attention and that the different ways in which a given issue might be understood in one context versus another are essentially unproblematic. Guided perhaps by the assumption that campaigns for human rights are essentially good things, more attention has been paid to the question of when they're most effective at achieving their objectives than to the more basic question of who defines what the objectives *are*.

Scholars such as Peggy Levitt and Sally Merry, in a helpful series of inquiries, insist on the importance of understanding the process of "vernacularization" through which global human rights concepts and tools are translated into local contexts. Their research explores the way ideas interact with one another, how concepts of rights reflected in international treatises interact with practices and dialogues in a given community; sometimes, they argue, this process works better than others. On one level, the story of Central American IP advocacy might be read as a case in which "vernacularization" didn't work. But on a deeper level, I suggest, it might lead us to question some underlying assumptions about the nature of these transnational campaigns.

As Levitt and Merry write, "Values packages land on and bounce off particular geographies rutted by history and culture. We could imagine how easily women's rights might travel if they circulated through unmarked, smooth terrains. But this is rarely the case" (Levitt and Merry 2009, 455). Yet such approaches seem to imply that human rights resides in its purest form at the global level, that it gets distorted—or even "polluted" (Levitt and Merry 2009, 454)—when it hits local realities. Somehow in this model, actors situated closer to the global level have more purchase on discerning what rights are, though they may not always be successful in making that resonate with local publics.

Yet the global road is rutted too. In Central American struggles over intellectual property, the challenge wasn't simply that international frames didn't layer well onto local realities (although that was also true). The deeper challenge was, and is, that there are many possible interpretations of how to operationalize human rights concepts, especially as regards social and economic rights like the right to health; differently situated actors have different abilities to advocate for their priority framings. Although Levitt and Merry suggest that the "magic" of human rights resides in its connection to the universal, that connection need not be drawn by transnational campaigners alone; local activists perceive it, too. In Central America, local health advocates were describing health as a human right and citing international agreements like the Declaration of Alma-Ata, or the International Covenant on Economic, Social, and Cultural Rights, long before the transnational IP advocates came to town. Yet because Oxfam and Doctors Without Borders were not focused on preserving participatory approaches to health or deepening the commitment to primary health care, the political opportunities that existed for implementing rights through such approaches were limited.

David Engel's essay on "Vertical and Horizontal Perspectives on Rights Consciousness" describes two paradigms for understanding the uptake, or lack thereof, of rights-based thinking in Global South societies. The dominant paradigm describes the diffusion of rights in vertical terms, "from what are conceived as higher, more powerful, prestigious or inclusive levels of legal organization to what are conceived of as lower, less powerful, and more localized levels"; the horizontal perspective, instead, looks for rights-talk within the broader context of shared meanings and interpretive practices employed by ordinary people. Engel argues that both approaches shed important light on the life of rights but that focusing exclusively on the vertical model can be misleading, tilting findings in favor of a top-down approach: "Liberal legalism is the active agent, and the societies of the global South are the potential recipients of this dynamic force. The question is therefore the readiness of actors in these societies to accept these legal practices and the conditions that are required for acceptance to occur. . . . The factors that prevent acceptance tend to be constructed negatively as irrational and undemocratic—such as 'Big Men,' despots or theocrats" (2012).

Engel emphasizes that in Thai society there are discourses for understanding injury outside the scope of rights that are often overlooked by scholars employing the more common vertical paradigm. In the case of Central American IP politics, instead of arguing that there are "rights-based" and "non–rights-based" discourses available to actors—though undoubtedly this is true—I emphasize that even in the "rights-based" category alone there are multiple possible interpretations of what *rights* means. Global transnational organizations may favor certain understandings, but these are not the only possible understandings nor necessarily the most transformative. A vertical perspective on intellectual property and rights struggles in Central America would suggest that the limited local uptake of IP was due to local culture or capacity impediments; indeed, I first approached this research assuming this to be the case. Over the course of my research, however, I learned that Central American health activists' visions of rights were equally rooted in global movements and agreements but that they actually have a more radical and transformative understanding of what a right to health means than the quintessentially neoliberal vision touted by transnational access advocates.

This view of Central American IP politics reveals that there is not one unitary axis along which rights flow up and down, becoming less "pure" and transformative as they encounter local realities. There are multiple imaginings of rights, and politics and power within and among transnational networks shape which ones rise to prominence at any given time (Carpenter 2007). If one particular imagining is more visible from our vantage point as researchers, this probably reflects our proximity to transnational activist circles more than it does anything inherently more transformative about that specific imagining.

As Mark Goodale writes, "In moving away from the global/local dichotomy . . . we must be cautious not to overprivilege the role of cosmopolitan elites, those 'activists without borders' whose very movements across both cultural and territorial boundaries seem to symbolize the normative transnationalism they advocate. . . . Many of the most important actors whose encounters with human rights discourse contribute to its transnationalism never physically leave their villages, or towns, or countries" (2007, 21–22). As we think, therefore, about the right to health, we might be mindful of adopting less top-down assumptions about the ways in which it is conceptualized.

And thirdly, this sort of campaigning invites questions about how we know what we're fighting for. On the one hand, as already noted, the tendencies evident in the access to medicines campaigns are a needed corrective to the neocolonialist tendencies of previous human rights campaigning critiqued by scholars such as Mutua and Kennedy. Mutua, in particular, argues that international human rights organizations focus on the practices of developing world leaders as "savages" whose practices need to be halted by enlightened "saviors" from the Global North. Kennedy, along similar lines, suggests that the intromission of human rights organizations ultimately undermines poor countries' efforts to handle their own problems in ways that reinscribe hierarchies of global power. Yet the campaigns for access to medicines are different. Typically they don't so much decry the errant practices of Global South governments as the strictures placed on them by supranational organizations, backed by Northern governments and corporations. In this sense, transnational access to medicines campaigners can rightfully argue they are working to empower rather than undermine Southern governments by altering the global economic order.

Yet, in some ways, these campaigns suffer from a different sort of myopia. While "traditional" human rights campaigning targets poor governments without addressing global power imbalances, contemporary trade justice work may target transnational structures without examining the ways local states need to be held accountable for the poor administration of existing resources. As discussed in Chapter 3, intellectual property protection does not occur in a vacuum; its impact will be minimized or expanded by the degree to which state actors exercise their roles responsibly. We need access to the black box of state decision making about drugs to truly ensure human rights outcomes—and if we don't have it, we should ask ourselves: What we are arguing for, anyway? Ultimately, the argument of access to medicines activists is reducible to a simple concept: Intellectual property is bad because it limits market competition to bring down prices. Yet this fits hand in glove with the market idolatry progressive Central American health activists have long struggled to resist. Absent any provision to ensure that the market mechanisms actually work—or, more to the point, that patients get the pills they need—have we reduced human rights to unfettered market access?

Chapter 5

Patient Advocacy and Access
to Medicines Litigation

"YOU CAN'T UNDERSTAND WHAT IT'S LIKE unless you've been through it," a member of the cancer patients' organization in Guatemala City told me, tears brimming in her eyes as she remembered her own experience. She glanced to the side for a moment, composing herself. A supportive family member chimed in: "Everything changes . . . even Christmas." Before cancer, he explained, Christmas is a time of joy; even those too poor to exchange gifts can share the excitement of window shopping or the pleasure of a good meal. But once you've been diagnosed with cancer, even though everyone around you wants to be happy through the holidays, all you can think about is survival.

That's why, she continued with renewed energy, access to medicines is everything: "Even though we are all going to die eventually, of course, we all want to do everything we can to just live a little bit longer. That's why the drugs are so important. Even if they can't cure us, they can help us live just a little bit longer."

And in this context, the tools and tactics of human rights take on particular relevance. In Guatemala, the patient group Heroes of Hope's motto is, "Cancer is synonymous with struggle, not with death." Indeed, for many of the patients I spoke with during my travels through Central America, the struggle itself confers a certain degree of dignity, as patients refuse to resign themselves to a health system in which their rights are regularly ignored. Patients' associations like Heroes of Hope offer advice about the strain placed on family members by the illness, accompaniment to doctor's appointments, or a home-cooked meal during a difficult time. Sometimes, they organize among themselves to help a patient get to the hospital, as there are those too poor to pay bus fare, others too weak to walk, and many too ashamed to burden their families by asking for help. They sponsor workshops to educate members, at which specialists share knowledge about the disease and guidance on how to navigate the health care system. Some of these meetings involve pep talks for patients accustomed to being treated with little respect by an overburdened and underfunded health system: "You have rights!" the association president instructed her audience at one such gathering I attended.

And though not all patients survive their ordeal, some score significant victories along the way by invoking human rights mechanisms. In Guatemala and Costa Rica, recent years have seen dramatic increases in successful access to medicines litigation brought by patients before domestic courts; at the inter-American level, the precedent-setting access to medicines case was brought by Salvadoran Odir Miranda.

In fact, as regards health rights in particular, a growing body of scholarship shows that, in many ways, courts across the so-called developing world, and particularly in Latin America, are playing a key role in delivering on the right to health by ensuring access to medicines (Hogerzeil et al. 2006, 305; Yamin and Gloppen 2011; Gauri and Brinks 2008). In this sense, the common assumption that human rights are somehow a Northern concept against which Southern countries in particular often come up short is particularly wrongheaded; especially in the United States, we have much to learn from our Southern neighbors about health as a human right.

Yet not all the lessons are unremittingly positive. In this chapter I examine the way that patients' struggles for access to medicines as a human right, refracted through the lens of an extraordinarily ill-functioning and illegitimate state, may offer limited solutions for specific individuals at the expense of a sustainable health system, thus undermining institutions' ability to promote the right to health.

This builds on ideas explored in previous chapters in this book. In Chapter 3, I suggested that arguments against intellectual property that focus exclusively on pricing—as most do—tackle only one impediment to the right to health; in countries where states lack capacity or political will to effectively regulate the drug market, blocking patents or test data protection may deny PhRMA some satisfaction but does little to ensure that patients get the drugs they need. Ultimately more state intervention in the economy—to create competitive markets—and more oversight of state purchasing decisions is needed to provide reliable access to safe drugs. In Chapter 4, I explained that in the context of long-standing struggles over health rights in the region, transnational anti-IP campaigns failed to resonate with progressives suspicious of the local generics industry. Absent efforts to ensure the drugs' safety or fair distribution, anti-IP campaigns risk reducing to promotion of market access for particular product, motivated more by the global battle against PhRMA than the locally rooted realities of Central America.

Similarly, this chapter explores the way a well-intentioned but limited human rights intervention in health can produce perverse outcomes. It too calls for greater attention to the context of state decision making in our thinking about human rights gains and losses. Through an analysis of Guatemalan health rights litigation, I argue here that, cast against a near total lack of confidence in the state, human rights mechanisms may take on an excessively individualist character in ways that collectively hollow out rather than enhance capacity, thus ultimately undermining the right to health.

My point here is not that human rights are not relevant, or worse yet that they are dangerous, in settings of low state capacity; quite the opposite—I believe the concept is of core importance in all societies. Yet rather than following blind faith in the liberatory character of rights promises or assuming their inherent opposition to the commodification of health, we must be alert to the way rights are being put into practice in concrete settings.

Access to Medicines Litigation in Central America: An Overview

Guatemala and Costa Rica have both experienced waves of access to medicines litigation in the last decade. In both countries, the trend appears to respond to recent developments lowering access to justice barriers that had traditionally impeded effective rights protection in these countries.

In Costa Rica, for example, Bruce Wilson explains that the 1989 Constitutional amendment creating a new chamber of the Supreme Court, known as the "Sala IV," created a legal opportunity structure (Wilson 2011, 132–154). By removing such barriers as the requirement of legal representation and the payment of legal fees, and accepting cases 365 days a year, even from claimants who do not make reference to specific points of law in their filing, the Sala IV has dramatically altered the protection of fundamental rights in Costa Rica. In Guatemala, the trend responds less to institutional reform of the courts than to the health rights advocacy of the human rights ombudsperson's office and patients' advocacy groups like Heroes of Hope, both of which combined to bring down barriers to entry; this is discussed in more detail in the following pages.[1]

The cases in Guatemala and Costa Rica conform to the contours of a general trend documented elsewhere (Hogerzeil et al. 2006, 305; Yamin and Gloppen 2011; Gauri and Brinks 2008). Responding to earlier scholars' concerns about whether courts could and would effectively uphold social rights, in recent years a number of comparative analyses of the forces shaping legal mobilization around health rights have responded with a resounding yes. In an analysis of seventy-one court cases from twelve countries in the Global South, Hogerzeil and his coauthors found that, particularly in Latin America, patients were successful in demanding access to essential medicines through litigation rooted in the right to health (Hogerzeil et al. 2006, 305). Gauri and Brinks's 2008 volume documents the frequency of successful right to health cases in India, South Africa, Brazil, Nigeria, and Indonesia, arguing that thousands of lives have been saved through such mechanisms. At the same time, their work begins to raise questions as to some of the perhaps unintended consequences, or less salutary implications, of such trends. Yamin and Gloppen's volume takes some of this reasoning a step further, asking such questions as who benefits from health rights claims and whether on balance they broaden access to medications for the population as a whole (Yamin and Gloppen 2011).

In Guatemala and Costa Rica, as in the other Latin American countries, these cases are filed as amparo[2] proceedings. Most Latin American Constitutions grant the right to amparo[3] as a specific means of protecting constitutional rights. In these cases, plaintiffs allege that the refusal to grant them access to medicines or treatments threatens their constitutional rights, including the right to health, and at times other rights (the right to social security or the right to life, for example). In many countries, these cases are strikingly successful; in the Costa Rican case, for example, Wilson reports that over 60 percent of amparos for access to medicines are granted by the court.

In Guatemala and Costa Rica, as in other civil law countries, a very high volume of access to medicines cases involve individual claimants, rather than collective petitioners or class action suits. In Brazil, for example, Ferraz (2009) reports that between 80 and 100 percent of cases involve individual plaintiffs. Most seek access to specific drugs or treatments. Many of these cases grant access to high-cost medications excluded from institutions' basic medications lists; although state drug authorities typically allow patients to petition for access to off-list drugs, such petitions are reviewed through an official process that patients frequently consider slow and unresponsive. By having access to the courts instead of relying on institutional review boards, patients secure more rapid access to their desired drugs.

In this chapter, I focus on the Guatemalan case, which has not been studied elsewhere. While it is not exceptional in its overall characteristics, I believe it merits our attention for a number of reasons. To begin with, Guatemala is certainly not a place where one would expect a "rights revolution." While most comparative scholars of social rights enforcement would likely agree with Gauri and Brinks that "One would expect . . . that substantial legalization will more often take place in relatively well-functioning democratic contexts" (Gauri and Brinks 2008), Guatemala's human rights record remains indisputably poor, and confidence in its judicial system, in particular, is abysmal. One recent analysis of the prospects for justice on rights claims before Guatemala's courts concluded that the Guatemalan justice system was "irreconcilably deficient"; as Davis and Warner write, "Both governmental agencies and non-governmental organizations (NGOs) monitoring the judiciary in Guatemala during and after the war have unanimously found that Guatemala's courts not only failed to offer citizens adequate judicial remedies, but actually aided human rights violations and perpetrated impunity" (Davis and Warner 2007, 7).

Beyond the courts, other institutions enjoy similarly low levels of confidence among the Guatemalan population. Surveys of citizen perception routinely rank the legitimacy of institutions in Guatemala among the lowest in the Western Hemisphere (Power and Cyr 2009, 253–272). The health sector, in particular, has been the subject of a number of high-profile corruption scandals in recent years. So, although health rights litigation has flourished in recent years, this is decidedly *not* indicative of a broad trend in the judicial enforcement of rights in Guatemala. Yet, if rights mechanisms are providing meaningful relief for everyday people in this unlikeliest of settings, this shows that rights operate unevenly not only across countries, but within them, calling out for further research into the complex forces shaping such trends and their implications in diverse contexts.

While it is often assumed that greater responsiveness to individual rights claims should increase the perceived legitimacy of public institutions, the Guatemalan case suggests that sometimes this may not work. Is there a threshold of legitimacy below which rights claims take on an excessively individualistic character given the near total lack of faith in public institutions? I return to this question after a description of the Guatemalan cases in the following section.

Documenting the Cases

To understand the trend of health rights litigation in Guatemala, I constructed a database of health rights cases since 2000, using several sources of information. First, in interviews with key actors including patients, attorneys, and public health officials, I asked about broad trends in litigation with which they were familiar; these conversations enabled me to come up with specific keywords, and sometimes specific case numbers and references, which I used to locate relevant cases on the Constitutional Court's online database of jurisprudence. The keywords used included the names of drugs, diseases, institutions involved in cases, names of patients' associations, and of specific individuals involved in cases. Second, attorneys from the human rights ombudsman's office (Procuraduría de los Derechos Humanos, known by its Spanish-language acronym, PDH) gave me case numbers for specific cases they had litigated, which I then looked up on the court's website. And, third, the court occasionally cites previous decisions in similar cases; in this way, I was able to obtain some snowball sampling as some cases referred me to others. Through all of these means, I compiled decisions from 271 cases, which I read and then reduced into a database of ninety-nine decisions in which patients had brought suit against public institutions for denial of their right to health through failure to provide access to medicines or treatment. I then coded these cases into five claim categories and analyzed them in terms of the motivations for bringing the case, illnesses involved, involvement of human rights officials, and timing of the case.

While I aimed to include all access to medications/treatment cases in the database, this was impossible for a number of reasons.[4] So, although the database represents an imperfect approximation of the total universe of access to medicines cases, I believe it is as accurate as can be produced under existing constraints and that it can be taken as loosely representative of the overall trend.

To shed further light on the dynamics behind the trend, I also conducted interviews with members of patients' associations, PDH lawyers, staff at IGSS (Instituto Guatemalteco de Seguridad Social, or Social Security Institute), and staff at the Constitutional Court. In the following discussion, I describe first the cases themselves and then the conversations I held with key informants about their implications.

Basic Characteristics of the Cases

The Guatemalan Constitution and laws are generous in their guarantees of health rights. Article 93 of the Constitution stipulates that health is a fundamental right of all human beings, and Articles 94 through 99 impose on the state a series of duties to ensure the health of the population. Article 100 establishes a right to social security for all inhabitants of the nation and mandates the funding of the IGSS through a tripartite structure including contributions from the state, from employers, and from workers. Health rights are further elaborated in the country's health code, which guarantees, in Article 4, access to health services free of charge for all those whose incomes make them unable to afford care otherwise.

Due to its constitutional mandate, the IGSS occupies a privileged status among Guatemalan health institutions and as a result is the primary party against whom citizens bring lawsuits for access to medicines. IGSS's functioning is governed by its own norms and regulations, many of which are challenged as unfair or overly lengthy by plaintiffs requesting protection from the courts. For example, as a means of cost containment, IGSS

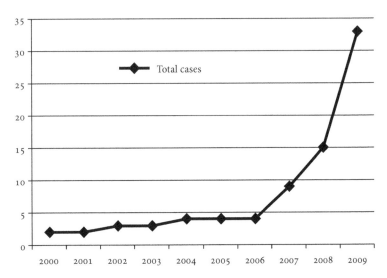

FIGURE 5.1. Total cases, by year.

maintains a basic list of approved medications. This list specifies appropriate therapies for conditions, based on determinations of drug safety, efficacy, and cost effectiveness. IGSS mandates a separate administrative procedure for the approved acquisition of particularly high-cost medications not on the basic list. In practice, patients and attorneys reported that the process of requesting access to a high-cost medication takes about six months to reach resolution. Therefore, many patients have turned to the courts as a means of both expediting that process and increasing their likelihood of positive results.

As Figure 5.1 shows, the volume of access to medicines cases has risen dramatically in recent years. In the overwhelming number of cases involving patients with access to medicines claims, the courts found in favor of the plaintiffs. In fact, by mid-2010 the volume of such cases had become unmanageable for IGSS, leading to the establishment of a working commission to handle such cases outside the courts.

On examination of the ninety-nine access to medication cases, a number of types emerge. In the following discussion, I offer categorization first by type of complaint (see Figure 5.2)—and second by the type of sickness for which relief was sought (see Figure 5.3).

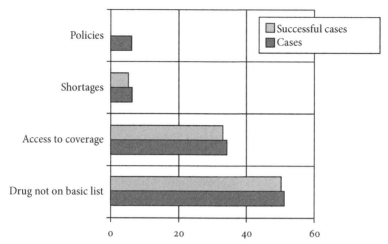

FIGURE 5.2. Types of cases.

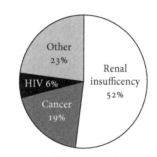

FIGURE 5.3. Diseases involved in cases.

As regards types of complaints, by far the largest category of cases—
fifty-one out of ninety-nine—were brought by *patients seeking access to
a specific drug that was not included on the basic list of approved medications.* In these cases, patients were receiving medications but alleged that
the drugs they received were not satisfactory for treatment of their condition. Most of these cases were brought by individual claimants, but some
involved groups of patients with the same disease, such as several decisions
in early 2010 involving groups of approximately fifty patients each who objected to the social security system's decision to change the drug with which

their ailment (renal insufficiency) was treated. Only one of the cases in this category was unsuccessful; in fifty out of fifty-one such cases, or 98 percent, the court upheld the patient's right to access the medication sought.

A second category of cases—thirty-four out of ninety-nine—involved *disputes about whether the patient in question was affiliated to the social security system or the duration of treatment to which an affiliated patient was entitled.* In many such cases, patients who required treatment for a chronic condition and lost their jobs during the course of treatment appealed to the courts for relief when the social security system attempted to deny them coverage. Others involved disputes about the duration of coverage for an individual patient whose affiliated status was not disputed.[5] Of these thirty-four cases in which patients disputed a denial or suspension of social security coverage, all but one, or 97 percent, of the plaintiffs were successful.

A much smaller category of cases—only six—involved charges of *rights violations due to a scarcity of available medications or treatments ("desabastecimiento").* In these cases, unlike the first category, patients were not receiving drugs or treatment at all, due to the ill-functioning of various of the health system's institutions. One of the five was a "diffuse interests" case brought on behalf of all patients in the social security system, alleging that the institution had failed to plan adequately, resulting in denials of access to medications across the board; the others involved groups of patients with specific illnesses. In five of the six cases, or 83 percent, the court upheld patients' claims and ordered the relevant institution to immediately address the shortage.

Lastly, a final set of six cases analyzed dealt with *policy disputes* rather than individual patients' access to specific drugs. These cases involved allegations that the authorities had adopted policies that were unconstitutional because they resulted in restricted access to medications and hence violations of the right to health. Half of these disputes pertained to specific policies governing the bidding process by which state institutions determined which drugs to buy, and half alleged the unconstitutionality of newly restrictive intellectual property laws. The Court did not rule in the plaintiffs' favor in any of these cases.

A total of ninety-two of the ninety-nine cases involved patients seeking access to specific medications or treatments; of these, forty-seven cases involved renal insufficiency; seventeen involved cancer (of which twelve were breast cancer, all of whom sought access to Herceptin); six involved HIV; three involved leukemia; and eighteen stemmed from other assorted illnesses. As already mentioned, many cases (especially renal cases) involved dozens of plaintiffs, and others invoked the general class of patients afflicted with the illness, so the number of cases should not be assumed to correspond to the number of patients affected by a given decision.

But Is This Good? A Closer Look at the Implications

Yet what are the social justice implications of this rising tide of individual rights cases? The literature on legalization of health rights has become increasingly (and appropriately) concerned with questions of equity and sustainability. The Guatemalan case underscores and expands these areas of concern. I address both aspects in order, as follows.

First, as regards *equity*, as Norheim and Wilson write in their analysis of Costa Rica, "To investigate the effects of litigation on priority setting and social justice, we need to know who benefits, in terms of patient groups, and the distribution of benefits: how much are these persons helped, compared to other patients in need?" (Norheim and Wilson 2010: 2). A number of studies suggest that most rights claims are brought by disproportionately middle-class patients (Ferraz 2009). This raises important questions about whether the existence of legal mechanisms granting access improves equity in health systems or merely reinforces existing social hierarchies, which largely determine who seeks justice through the courts. Although the socioeconomic status of the petitioners is not a primary focus of my inquiry here, the mere fact that the overwhelming majority (in my database, ninety of ninety-nine cases) are brought against the Guatemalan Social Security Institute, which—as discussed in Chapter 3—insures only a relatively privileged segment of the population, suggests that similar dynamics may be in effect in Guatemala.

Second, the findings from these studies also point to concerns about *sustainability*. Namely, does granting patients a means by which to advocate for particular drugs on the basis of individual rights—effectively circumventing institutional mechanisms to assess the cost effectiveness of treatment—distort the spending priorities of health systems? For example, Norheim and Gloppen argue that "resources are often allocated to fund costly treatments that provide only marginal health benefits for severe conditions" (Norheim and Gloppen 2011, 329). Given the reality of scarce resources, this enforcement of the right to health can undermine needed mechanisms for institutional priority setting by mandating the purchase of drugs that do not meet the cost effectiveness criteria used by public health agencies. What's more, because such purchases are mandated piecemeal—for individual patients as ordered by the courts, rather than as an institutional decision that can be budgeted and planned for—purchases are usually not made through a competitive bidding process, which likely contributes to higher pricing.

The Guatemalan experience underscores the importance of this question. Of the fifty-one Guatemalan cases where patients who were receiving medications appealed to the courts because they desired a *different* medication, most involved patients who did not want to take the generic medication provided by the social security system, preferring an originator drug. There are two ways that such cases came about: first, when a patient started out on a brand-name drug and resisted being switched to a generic, which occurred in just over half of the fifty-one cases (twenty-eight cases); and second, when a patient believed that a drug she had not yet tried would be better than the generic drug she was taking, which occurred in nineteen cases. I discuss each of these two types of cases in the following subsections.

Cases in Which the Patient Resisted a Change of Medication

In twenty-seven cases, patients who had already taken an originator drug expressed concern that IGSS was requiring them to change drugs for reasons external to their health needs—in other words, for cost reasons. These patients had initiated treatment using a brand-name drug either because they had initially paid for it out of pocket or received it as a donation or because IGSS had in previous years purchased the drug in its brand-name form but subsequently decided to switch to a lower-cost provider (perhaps when an originator's patent expired or a new generic alternative entered the market). In both of these types of cases, the court typically upheld the patient's right to continue on his or her previously prescribed medication regimen. In this sense, once a patient had initiated treatment on a given drug regimen, the court favored the status quo.

For example, Felipe Augusto Estrada had had a renal transplant and was receiving ongoing treatment at IGSS. In 2006 he reported that he was not responding as desired to the regimen of generic drugs (ciclosporina, prednisona, and micofenolato mofetil) that IGSS's doctors had prescribed to him, so he chose to buy Novartis's Certican on the private market using his own funds and found it to be preferable. When he requested Certican by brand name at the IGSS hospital, he was told that he would need to follow IGSS's preestablished procedures for requesting access to high-cost medications, but he considered these too time consuming given the fragility of his health. For this reason, he filed an amparo, and the Constitutional Court upheld a lower court's ruling in his favor, arguing that the failure to provide him with Certican, the medication that had been shown to be effective in his case, represented an imminent threat to his health and indeed his life. IGSS was therefore required to provide him with immediate access to Certican.

Similarly, in one 2008 case, twenty-two patients with chronic renal insufficiency who had been receiving Cellcept, manufactured by the Swiss drugmaker Roche, reported that in recent months the social security system had provided them with a bioequivalent alternative produced by an Indian generic producer, sold under the trade name Refrat. Some of the patients reported having experienced diarrhea, dehydration, and increased creatine levels as a result of the switch in medication; citing a previous case in which other patients were granted, via amparo, access to a drug they had come to trust, these patients argued that they should continue to receive Cellcept. Representatives of IGSS, on the other hand, argued that the generic drug had provided proof of its bioequivalence to Cellcept and had cleared all the requirements of the institution as regards evidence of its effectiveness and safety. Furthermore, when nephrologists were consulted on the case, they stated that the patients who had reported adverse effects to the new drug had also reported similar side effects to the previous drug;[6] therefore, they argued, there was no scientific basis by which to attribute their symptoms to the generic drug alone.

The Constitutional Court ruled in favor of the petitioners, writing:

> Given the doubts regarding the suitability of administering the medication to which the petitioners object, of trade name Refrat, versus the

brand name medication Cellcept which they had always received, the refusal to continue providing the petitioners with the solicited medication
implies a direct personal offense and results in the violation of the rights
guaranteed in Constitutional articles 3, 93, 95, and 100; the 4th article,
number 1 of the Inter-American Convention on Human Rights; the 6th
Article, number 1 of the International Covenant on Civil and Political
Rights; and the 12th Article of the International Covenant on Social,
Economic, and Cultural Rights . . . For this reason, this Court consid-
ers that the appeal should be upheld . . . for the effect of preventing the
eventual violation of the right to life and to health of the petitioners, and
so that they might continue enjoying the administration of the medication that their illness requires, and which had been provided to them
previously by the Guatemalan Social Security Institute, until such time
as there is medical certainty about the change of medication. (Corte de
Constitucionalidad de Guatemala 2008)

These two cases are illustrative of a broader trend. The Court frequently
accepts patients' arguments that they have a right to continue a treatment
once initiated; even if such treatment was initiated using private funds,
or under the authority of a different medical institution, the courts have
found that the social security system has a corresponding duty to assume
the costs of its continuance. This favoring of the status quo as regards treatment does not appear to be unique to Guatemala; Hogerzeil and his coauthors note that almost one-fifth of the cases reviewed involved "acquired
rights, in the sense of non-interruption of treatment already supplied for a
period of time" (Hogerzeil et al. 2006, 305). This has clear budgetary implications because originator drugs are typically orders of magnitude more
costly than generic alternatives. Furthermore, these implications become
more worrisome under the provisions of intellectual property law. When
patents or test data exclusivity expire, generic drugs may enter the market,
but if state agencies are legally blocked from switching patients onto more
cost-effective alternatives as they become available, the result approaches a
permanent monopoly for brand-name drugs. Effectively, the monopoly is
upheld during the patent period by intellectual property law and following
its expiry by human rights law.

Patients Demanding First-Time Access to Brand-Name Drugs

The aforementioned effect is further reinforced if new patients receiving drugs for the first time can appeal to the courts to ensure they are granted access to the more expensive brand-name drugs even if they have not previously taken such drugs. There is evidence that this, too, occurs. In eighteen of the fifty-one medications cases studied, patients sought access to drugs they had not previously taken but that they believed would be preferable to the drugs available to them under the IGSS's basic list. In many cases, patients were told about specific high-cost drugs by patients' associations or by their own doctors; when IGSS refused to provide them those drugs, they turned to the courts. In some cases, patients report having been told at the hospital that the drug they sought was available only to patients who were covered by an amparo mandating its provision (see, for example, case 2054-2009). In my own participation in the meetings of one patients' association, I observed patients sharing strategies and contacts for the amparo filing process as a means of rapid access to originator drugs. The drug company whose funds had underwritten the meeting in question, and whose products were featured in literature placed at every participant's seat, was prominently represented in this discussion.

In these cases, the Court upheld patients' rights not just to treatment, but to a *specific* medication, barring its substitution with other drugs or treatments. For example, in the 2009 case of breast cancer patient Yesenia Rocío Barrios Rodas, the Court ordered provision of Herceptin (trastuzumab), forbidding its substitution with other drugs unless the patient's doctors recommend them as superior:

> Although the IGSS may obtain other products which it considers to be ideal on a scientific and determined basis for the treatment of its members, it cannot vary from the provision of the medicine mentioned by the Human Rights Ombudsman in the case of Yesenia Rocío Barrios Rodas, unless it has a medical diagnosis which indicates the need for its suspension or change; and hence, unless it has another drug which has characteristics identified as superior to those of the aforementioned drug. (2883-2009)

It is noteworthy that, under this ruling, substitution requires a medical finding of drug superiority, not simply equivalency.

State Legitimacy and Human Rights

In Guatemala, two institutions have played a key role in making judicial relief accessible for everyday citizens who lack access to medicines. First, the office of the human rights ombudsman (PDH) made a specific commitment to take health rights claims seriously. The ombudsman himself, Sergio Morales, has intervened prominently in a number of key cases in recent years and instructed the attorneys on his staff to provide legal representation for patients seeking access to medicines. Because the PDH takes cases free of charge, and the ombudsman's involvement confers legitimacy on cases, virtually all of my interviewees familiar with the justice system agreed that the PDH's intervention both inaugurated the trend of health rights cases and made this form of effective rights protection accessible to all Guatemalans. In the overwhelming majority of Guatemalan amparo cases, plaintiffs are represented by attorneys from the PDH.

Similarly, patients' associations have played a key role in reducing barriers to access for key populations. They support patients through the amparo process, explaining what sort of documentation will be required by the PDH and helping them gather the required information. Although association members told me that some lawyers at the PDH were responsive and understanding, this was not a universal trait, and many lamented that most patients' lack of confidence in the legal system often leads them to be reluctant to go through with a claim unless supported and encouraged by the association. In addition, some court decisions have granted drugs to patients who are members of specific associations—and not to patients who are not—thus granting the association a key gatekeeping role. In interviews with PDH lawyers, they also reported a higher degree of confidence in the validity and seriousness of claims coming from individuals affiliated with patient groups.

In my interviews with patients and lawyers involved in health rights litigation of this sort, some common threads emerged. First, all agreed that health, as a human right, should not be subjected to financial considerations. They argued this both on principle and because, in practice, they felt their government's health institutions were untrustworthy. One member of a patients' association told me the ultimate affront was the social security institute's decision to determine access to high-cost medicines based on a cost-benefit analysis. "Cost-benefit!" he declared, his voice trembling with rage. "This is a trampling of human dignity, a violation of the right to health, a mockery of humanity." Without exception, they rejected provisions designed to reduce costs by limiting access.

Another patient took offense at the statement, in the social security institute's policy, that high-cost therapies would be provided for patients whose lives would be "useful and productive" as a result of their having access to the drug: "So if you're stuck in bed and can't work, your life has no value?"

Across the board, they spoke with grave concern about health systems' decisions to use generic drugs as a cost-saving measure. Most used the terms *generic* and *low-quality* interchangeably; when I asked them to clarify what they meant, a frequent response was, "These are drugs that have no clinical studies" (a fact that is, of course, true of all generics but doesn't necessarily mean they are of poor quality). Many underscored the seriousness of the matter by adding that some of these medicines were from Asia; one Guatemalan patient leader told me she might, under some circumstances, be willing to accept a generic drug from the United States or Europe but not from Central America and certainly not from India, "because our lives are worth just as much as people's lives in the developed countries."

When I asked many patients why, if concerned about quality, they argued for access to specific brand name drugs rather than effective quality-control mechanisms that would ensure the safety of all drugs. They responded that they had no confidence in their government's ability to ensure quality in a transparent and independent manner—"I wouldn't trust the state," one patient told me. "Not here in Guatemala."

While lawyers at the PDH addressed these issues in a more dispassionate manner, they too rejected the notion that health should be held hostage to financial considerations, for many of the same reasons. When I asked them whether the net result of so many cases granting individual access to high-cost medications might make it harder for the IGSS to budget adequately for other services, thus undermining the right to health, they expressed deep skepticism that the IGSS could be trusted to spend the money appropriately in any event. Most everyone mentioned the deep corruption scandals that have rocked the IGSS in recent years—while the charges that

US$45 million went missing during the recent presidency of Alfonso Portillo provide the most sensational scandal, most seemed to suspect that the siphoning off of public resources continued apace today.

And this skepticism puts them in good company: According to Transparency International's Corruption Perception Index, in 2008 Guatemala's corruption was "serious," only one-tenth of a point outside the range designated as "rampant" (Ruhl 2011, 33–58). Similarly, in response to the 2009 Latinobarómetro survey question, "Imagine that there are 100 public employees in the country and you have to say how many you believe are corrupt. How many would you say are corrupt?" Guatemala's average answer was 76.2, indicating extremely low levels of confidence in public institutions (Ruhl 2011, 33–58). As one of the human rights lawyers told me, "I might feel differently if they [IGSS] weren't a bunch of thieves to begin with."

On the one hand, it may be tempting to dismiss these arguments by assuming that patients' associations and their allies are captives of private commercial interests. Indeed, it has been well documented that patients' associations around the world often have strong ties to pharmaceutical corporations; increasingly, studies have documented a connection between patient groups' sources of financial support and their stance on policy issues (Perehudoff and Alves 2011; Hemminki, Toiviainen, and Vuorenkoski 2010, 1171–1175; Jones 2008, 929–943; Lofgren 2004, 228). A number of these studies have also shown that many patient groups did not fully disclose the extent of their relationship with the pharmaceutical industry despite legal obligations to do so, suggesting deliberate deception (Perehudoff and Alves 2011; Hemminki, Toiviainen, and Vuorenkoski 2010, 1171–1175). Corporate accountability advocates have argued that the ties Big PhRMA has built with patients' groups are part of an "astroturf" public relations strategy, in which corporate funding generates the appearance of grassroots support that can then be mobilized to defend corporate interests (Burton and Rowell 2003; Gerth and Stolberg 2000).

In Guatemala, too, evidence of such connections is easy to find. I attended a meeting of one patients' association in which all participants were treated to a meal and a lecture about the latest drugs, sponsored by a pharmaceutical company that placed literature touting the drugs at each attendee's seat. Yet, despite this, it is overly simplistic to reduce the patient groups I spoke with to front groups for PhRMA. Many, in fact, were at least moderately critical of pharmaceutical companies, suggesting their donations, while appreciated, were minimal in proportion to their profits. All were focused on their patients' very real struggle for survival; in countries where the safety of the drug supply is not assured, it is understandable that many see the fight to stay alive as a fight for access to originator drugs, which are assumed to be safer. Many patients told me of specific instances where generic medications, despite having been approved by IGSS, appeared to be ineffective. Although some of the patients' allegations are disputed by IGSS and generic company representatives as lacking scientific validity, some claims struck me as compelling; for example, patients in one organization told me they noticed that when given a specific generic pill, they defecated the pill whole. Given that the medicine involved was to treat a life-threatening condition, and the pill emerged from their digestive system intact, this caused understandable alarm.

Similarly, the disturbingly regular occurrence of high-profile theft and corruption scandals within IGSS contributes to a climate of public skepticism surrounding the integrity of the institution's decision-making process. For individuals facing life-threatening illnesses in any country, some degree of skepticism about the intentions of their health service providers is reasonable, even perhaps recommended; in Guatemala, given the absence of a transparent and legitimate system to ensure the safety and effectiveness of the drug supply and the fair distribution of public funds, the allure of an amparo process with almost certain guarantees of positive resolution for plaintiffs is not at all surprising. In this context, one need not be in the pocket of pharmaceutical corporations to seek out available remedies in the interest of survival.

Conclusions

The proliferation of these cases would appear to have introduced the possibility of a perverse role for human rights reasoning in health systems. Ironically, the availability and apparent enforcement of individual rights claims for specific drugs creates a system whereby brand-name pharmaceutical companies can extend the initial market exclusivity ensured them through intellectual property law almost indefinitely. For all of the optimism that human rights mechanisms might serve as a mechanism to ensure equity in health (Yamin 2010) or even a check on monopolistic tendencies of intellectual property law (Forman 2008, 37), it would seem that in these concrete cases the opposite occurs. Under such a system, human rights risks becoming the mechanism whereby private corporations head off competition, ensuring themselves a lucrative and exclusive market and charging taxpayers for the privilege.

Of course, there is nothing inherent in human rights reasoning to produce this perverse outcome. As Lisa Forman demonstrates, public health advocates often invoke human rights arguments in demanding flexibilities in intellectual property rules that limit access to affordable medications, and have achieved some success in doing so (Forman 2008, 37). As Yamin argues, "The real question for health rights . . . is not so much a question of remedying specific violations as changing decision-making processes to incorporate prospectively an equity lens, which goes beyond health specifically to also contemplate other social determinants, from fiscal to labor to land policy" (Yamin 2011: 369). Furthermore, Yamin argues persuasively that courts *can* push forward broader societal discussion of these issues and prompt far-reaching health sector reforms, citing the Colombian Constitutional Court's T-760/08 decision, which called for universal coverage and ordered structural reforms to reduce inequalities in the health system (Yamin 2011). Gloppen and Roseman also assert that in Argentina, Brazil, and Colombia courts have adopted landmark decisions on public interest cases brought by local NGOs (Gloppen and Roseman 2011, 1–16).

Yet the experience of Guatemala suggests similar judgments are unlikely in this context. Indeed, in Guatemala the Constitutional Court heard, but ultimately rejected, rights-based arguments for the unconstitutionality of CAFTA because of the projected impact of its intellectual property provisions on access to medicines; by contrast, it has overwhelmingly favored the claims of individual patients seeking access to specific medications, even where granting such claims risks imperiling the rights of unknown others from whom resources must be reallocated given the reality of finite budgets. This is ultimately unsurprising, as courts tend to favor individual cases of identifiably suffering plaintiffs over abstract injustices wrought by unduly burdened institutional budgets; as Barrett and her coauthors write, "When new technologies arise, it is relatively easy to pit the known patient in need against either the system in general or a set of 'anonymous' patients elsewhere" (2006, 1118–1120).

Ultimately, my argument here that such cases may have the net result of undermining rational planning and priority-setting in health systems is not new; similar concerns have been raised in other contexts. Yet the Guatemalan cases provide a particularly apt illustration of the way such tendencies intersect with intellectual property law. Because a significant proportion of patients are granted ongoing rights to originator drugs through human rights mechanisms, even when generic versions are legally available on the market, human rights law may have the perverse effect of extending patent life. Far from a check on the power of the patent system as envisioned by Forman, human rights reasoning may be the very vehicle through which its power is enhanced and extended.

This occurs in part because of the Guatemalan courts' decision to assume that patients have an absolute right to the medicine prescribed by their attending physician. Yamin (2011, 361–362) argues that this interpretation, while common in the Latin American context, is problematic, especially given physicians' demonstrated vulnerability to economic incentives that affect their prescribing decisions. However, in Guatemala a second factor underpins these judgments. The state's lack of capacity and/ or political will to ensure the safety of the drug supply makes patients' and physicians' insistence on originator drugs less specious than it would otherwise be, rendering the courts' reluctance to accept generic substitution reasonable, through the narrow lens of what's best for the individual patient before them.

In this sense, the Guatemalan case is different from that of other more developed Global South nations. Although many access to medicines cases unfold against the backdrop of negligent and apparently uncaring state bureaucracies, many riddled with corruption scandals, the argument for a human right to originator drugs is much weaker in cases where generics can be proven safe and effective. Where even that basic guarantee is lacking, not only are markets less competitive (as argued in Chapter 3), and civil society groups, even progressive ones, less interested in promoting generics (as argued in Chapter 4), but the courts too tend to understand patients' rights in a more limited and individualistic fashion, as I have argued here.

Human rights law—like the boomerang of transnational advocacy, which is most effective when focused on stopping the infliction of deliberate harm rather than undoing invisible systemic wrongs—is best equipped to understand us as individuals whose rights are threatened by states. But its use to uphold such social and economic rights as the right to health requires bolstering rather than restraining states. In contexts where states' legitimacy is as weak as Guatemala, human rights advocacy may produce the perverse outcome of a further gutted state, with even less control of its limited resources, less capacity to meet expectations, and less legitimacy in the eyes of the population.

Chapter 6

Writing Globalization's Rule Book

S O WHERE DO THESE EXPLORATIONS TAKE US, in terms of our understanding of the transformative potential of human rights? While the
foregoing chapters have afforded an opportunity to explore interesting empirical puzzles that arise in the context of contestation of health as a
human right, the underlying question this book seeks to answer is whether
human rights—as a discourse and set of practices—is up to the challenge
of confronting economic power. If not, are rights ultimately little more
than a fig leaf for economic exploitation?

The debates over intellectual property and the right to health, I have
argued, provide a privileged vantage point from which to examine this
question. For as the case studies sketched in these pages have revealed, the
battles over how to ensure access to medicine tap into two contrasting narratives for how best to order our globalized world: free trade and human
rights. As argued in Chapter 2, although both narratives emerged from
similar intellectual and political traditions and traversed somewhat parallel trajectories in their early years, "free" traders' unanticipated embrace
of selected protectionist principles, like IP, coupled with the human rights
movement's latter-day enthusiasm for the right to health, have led us to a
showdown: When both free trade and human rights advocates lay claim
to legitimate authority in IP and access decision making, who wins? Can
rights truly trump economic power?

Yet the question itself rests on the implicit assumption of opposition between these two camps. In this concluding chapter, I knit together insights from previous chapters to examine this assumed opposition more critically. I argue that, in fact, rights approaches often strengthen rather than contest existing hierarchies of power but that they need not do so: Our central challenge as rights advocates may lie in discerning when and how rights approaches have the greatest potential to transform existing asymmetries of power and deploying them more frequently along those lines. I conclude with some suggestions about how we might rethink our understandings of how rights work, based on the research in this book.

Human Rights as the Handmaiden of Market Rule?

As the global human rights movement strives increasingly to engage with social and economic rights such as the right to health, humanitarian organizations like Oxfam or Doctors Without Borders increasingly embrace the human rights framework to advance their efforts. There is, therefore, considerable optimism in some quarters about the use of the tried-and-true human rights "boomerang" against new targets.

For example, as health rights advocate Claudio Schuftan writes, "The value added flowing from the new human rights-based framework [in health] is the *legitimization* of such claims, giving them a politico-legal thrust" (2007, emphasis mine). The effort to demand access to medicines as a human right, and to mobilize for it in the courts and on the streets of Central America, is a clear test of this principle: In framing opposition to CAFTA as a defense of basic human rights rather than, say, opposition to imperialism, activists hope to use the legitimacy of the human rights discourse to draw a line that "free" trade cannot cross. Schuftan explains the attraction of the idea, writing, "Human rights . . . give direction and boundaries to contemporary political and economic choices: some economic choices are simply not permissible even if they promise a good return (e.g. slavery)" (2007).

Perhaps the human right to health, then, can hem in capital on the matter of intellectual property, as a number of authors have suggested (Forman 2008, 37; Helfer and Austin 2011). Indeed, successful past battles over access to medicines, particularly in South Africa, are often cited as illustrations of the way human rights tools can be deployed against the wrongs wrought by globalization (Klug 2008; Nelson and Dorsey 2003). In this sense, some scholars suggest, human rights can pose a potent challenge to prevailing economic arrangements.

On the other hand, however, the discourse of human rights can also be mobilized to defend the powerful. And indeed, the positioning of intellectual property itself as a "human right" provides a paradigmatic example of this. While the Universal Declaration of Human Rights and the International Covenant on Economic, Social, and Cultural Rights specifically recognize the rights of authors and inventors to enjoy the fruits of their innovation, the exact dimensions of these protections have yet to be clarified in law. The concept is nonetheless mobilized by defenders of intellectual property such as Robert Anderson and Hannu Wager, who argue in a recent article, "The World Trade Organization (WTO) has sometimes been portrayed as being at odds with the protection of human rights. This article takes issue with this perception . . . The rules and procedures of the WTO are directly supportive of civil rights in the sense of freedom to participate in markets and freedom from arbitrary governmental procedures" (Anderson and Wager 2006, 1).

As Larry Helfer warns, "Without greater normative clarity . . . such 'rights talk' risks creating a legal environment in which every claim (and therefore no claim) enjoys the distinctive protections that attach to human rights" (Helfer 2007, 976). Indeed, as Costas Douzinas writes, human rights have become a global lingua franca, "adopted by left and right, the north and the south, the state and the pulpit, the minister and the rebel. This is the discourse that makes them the only ideology in town, the ideology after the end of ideologies, the ideology at the end of history" (Douzinas 2007). But if everyone believes in human rights, has the term become an empty signifier?

This study finds evidence for both interpretations of rights—but, fundamentally, it suggests caution before we embrace rights as inherently liberatory (or inherently oppressive).

For example, I argue in Chapter 3 that, on scratching the surface of the access to medicines arguments offered in the course of CAFTA's ratification, what emerges are arguments that are about access to *markets*. Some IP critics' arguments risk reifying a misplaced faith in market mechanisms as adjudicators of access. In fact, I insist, in markets of limited competitiveness and virtually no effective regulation, it's not clear that IP is the central impediment to market-driven price drops, nor is it clear that, if IP barriers were removed, state purchasing would gravitate to low-cost generics. What's needed, in this context, is a hard look at the role of the state in both regulation and purchasing of drugs. While local health advocates have long called for greater state accountability along these and other lines, transnational campaigners have by and large sidestepped such debates, offering in their stead arguments that unwittingly prop up, rather than challenge, market idolatry.

In Chapter 4, I argue that this apparent disconnect between Central American and transnational activists led to short-lived and fragile alliances during the battle against CAFTA. Local activists bristled at the notion of aligning with industry to advocate for access to market for generics, for many reasons: because they were trained to approach health through the lens of social inequality and justice and to see market-based arguments with suspicion, because generic producers had historically opposed many efforts aimed at equity, and because, ultimately, many Central American health professionals expressed concern about the quality of at least some generic drugs, and the commitment of at least some drug producers, to access. In this context, I suggest, the arguments offered by transnational health activists may have been less counterhegemonic than those invoked by Central Americans.

Chapter 5 further shows that human rights can be invoked by other actors—in this case, patients' rights organizations and lawyers working for the human rights ombudsman—in ways that may in fact render the responsible resolution of long-term access questions more, rather than less, difficult for health institutions. Again, I suggest that vital state functions are performed so poorly in at least some Central American countries that court decisions made in the name of individual patients' rights may wind up reinforcing the logic of intellectual property, granting an indefinite extension on patents.

In all of these ways, then, the arguments offered by access advocates sound suspiciously like those of market triumphalists. Far from serving as a check on market sovereignty, human rights can be utilized in ways that serve effectively as its handmaiden.

A critical review of human rights history in the Americas suggests that perhaps we ought not be surprised by these findings. There are many ways in which human rights arguments nestle cozily with political-economic views that have been used to justify the status quo. After all, historically human rights have presented a particular view of the state and its obligations to its citizens, one that has trained far more attention on states as culprits of rights violations than crafters of social justice; the focus has been on reining states in rather than empowering them to act more aggressively. Paul Farmer warns that such an approach can effectively blind us to structural violence, which is the predominant cause of ill health. If we define extrajudicial executions as violent and mandate their cessation, yet tolerate mortality from preventable childhood disease rather than insisting on its eradication, our understanding of rights and our ability to bring about a better world are impoverished.

And not only structural violence but physical acts of violence as well can get misread through such a selective view of rights, as historian Greg Grandin (2004, 2005) warns. Indeed, Grandin suggests, the dominant reading of twentieth-century democratic history in Latin America—one in which democracy triumphs over dictatorship thanks to the unrelenting efforts of civil and political rights advocates—may eclipse some of the ways that rights struggles were always about social and economic justice as well as freedom from torture or state-sponsored execution. By defining twentieth-century Latin American dictatorships as dark descents into tyranny, strictly demarcated in time and detached from the much longer history of popular struggles for social reform, the human rights frame[1] construes Cold War violence as the aberrant and incomprehensible result of individual tyrants' wrath. In fact, Grandin (2004) suggests that these Cold War regimes might be productively understood as an effective counterrevolution, a deliberate attempt to roll back rights secured in reformist constitutions written at mid-century. Across the continent, Grandin argues, dictatorships arose in reaction to dramatic and hard-fought gains for labor, education, health, and other social aims. These were the culmination of decades of struggle and represented an affront to the interests of the entrenched elite who would later support—tacitly or openly—military dictatorships.

In this sense, the authoritarian regimes' actions are not unlike previous (and subsequent) waves of state violence aimed at quelling movements for popular democracy in the region. Yet human rights campaigns, in their focus on discrete, outrage-generating acts, run the risk of isolating reprehensible actions from their broader social, political, or historical context. The portrait of steel-jawed generals trampling the rights of cowering innocents may generate the Northern sympathies necessary for effective transnational action—in fact, Keck and Sikkink's (1998) research suggests this is precisely the trope used in the most successful transnational campaigns—but it ultimately sacrifices a more contextualized view grounding rights advancement in long-term social struggles for social justice. It also reframes protagonists in those long-term struggles as victims of state violence rather than advocates of social transformation (Kennedy 2004).

In fact, many, if not most, of those singled out by repressive regimes of the 1970s and 1980s across Latin America were targeted precisely because they were involved in efforts to craft or demand state policies aimed at public investment in social welfare, wealth redistribution, or other measures of social justice, many of them inspired by socialist ideals. The vision they sought to advance was one of state involvement in the promotion of social and economic, as well as political, rights. Yet when reprisals against them were reframed in civil rights terms more palatable to Northern sponsors, the killings of advocates of literacy or public health or clean water were described in ways that focused on the killings, not on their campaigns for literacy, or public health, or clean water. In the language of human rights, the state was thus recast as the entity that deprived citizens of their rights rather than the entity through which citizens were to secure their rights.[2]

Ironically, then, in appealing for assistance in language that resonated with U.S. or European definitions of "human rights," twentieth-century Latin American reformers tacitly acceded to the replacement of these more vibrant imagined democracies rooted in broad guarantees of social justice with more enervated substitutes reduced to individual rights against the state. Of course, this pared-down view of rights meshed with the foreign policy paradigm promoted by the U.S. government. Although Northern Hemisphere human rights organizations achieved some autonomy from the U.S. foreign policy establishment during the mid- to late twentieth century (Dezalay and Garth 2006), they did so while advancing a vision of rights rooted deeply in the liberal antistatist worldview that served (and serves) as the core U.S. justification for the forestalling of social and economic rights. Ironically, then, human rights discourse and practice during this period may have paved the way for the economic evisceration of state institutions that came with the "return" to democracy.[3] Human rights served as the handmaiden of free trade.

Cast against this history, we should perhaps be skeptical about expecting human rights protections to serve as an effective safeguard against the abuses of capital. On an empirical level, the mixed results of the cases reviewed in the foregoing chapters suggest that we should be cautious before putting too much stock in such a strategy. On a theoretical level, too, I believe that the promise of traditional liberal rights in resolving the challenges embedded in the contemporary intellectual property regime is limited. Yet the recognition of this fact brings us to an important precipice, from which it is possible to imagine new alternatives for social transformation.

My point here is not to assail liberal rights as useless for progressive politics; quite the contrary, I have spent too much time with courageous Central American activists who credit their very survival through death threats (and worse) to the classic letter-writing campaigns[4] to be able to make such a charge. Rather, I believe that the ground on which such rights are intended to operate is shifting beneath our feet, in ways that expose the entrenched weaknesses of a traditional liberal rights approach and invite a rethinking of tactics.

The Liberal Vision and Its Limitations

The theoretical underpinnings of liberal democracy rest on a number of assumptions that hold less and less true today, as our world experiences important changes associated with globalization, summarized in the following discussion. The story of liberal rights, of course, goes something like this: Autonomous individuals, endowed with rights by their Creator, surrender some minimum of these liberties in exchange for the basic order in which to make their lives. The imagined social contract that springs from this rational transaction forms the basis for state legitimacy—and the preexisting individual rights on which it is premised serve as a check on state excesses. This system has always had its limitations, and they have been expounded on elsewhere with eloquence and insight that exceed my own. I would like to take up only two of these critiques.

State-centrism

First, the tale is premised on the centrality of the state and citizens' rights against it: As Hannah Arendt notes and Giorgio Agamben later expands, there is a disjuncture between universal rights granted by virtue of one's humanity and a world in which nation-states provide rights protections for citizens, as the plight of refugees and stateless persons makes clear. As Agamben writes, "In the system of the nation-state, the so-called sacred and inalienable rights of man show themselves to lack every protection and reality at the moment in which they can no longer take the form of rights belonging to citizens of a state" (1998, 126). Efforts at constructing universal jurisdiction are an attempt to address this problem, but even these do not go far enough to remedy it, for they often seek to compensate for one state's failure to protect rights by appealing to another's, rather than transcending states.[5]

While some states' reluctance to hold their own former tyrants accountable is indeed a problem, arguably a greater one as we look ahead is states' limited control of corporate rights violators. If rights offer limited safeguards against the abuses of states, they have shown themselves dramatically less useful against the abuses of capital. And these are the paradigmatic abuses against which we need to fashion new tools.

As many scholars have argued (Castells 2000; Drahos and Braithwaite 2003; Robinson 1996, 2003, 2004; Sklair 2000), recent decades have seen profound changes to the global economy that reconfigure the relationships of populations to nation-states. Today, we find ourselves in an incomplete transition away from a world system based on the ever-increasing integration of national economies toward a truly global economy where production itself is a transnational process (Castells 2000; Robinson 2004). Under previous epochs, capitalist systems organized within nation-states to exchange with others; the nation-state was the dominant unit of analysis and played an important role as the primary site of contestation over the ways in which wealth was to be distributed. The current period is different, not because the volume of international transactions has increased but rather because these transactions themselves have transcended the "international" framework. The forces of production themselves are no longer contained within nation-states; to an unprecedented degree, both capital and labor have become mobile, liberated from the confines of national laws.[6] William Robinson (2004) and Leslie Sklair (2000) have argued that, as a result, we are witnessing the rise of a transnational capitalist class, defined as such because "it is tied to globalized circuits of production, marketing, and finances unbound from particular national territories and identities and because its interests lie in global over local or national accumulation" (Robinson 2004).[7] As a result, representatives of this class in different countries work to articulate the national state ever more into global economic and political circuitry and to inscribe it into the emergent legal system being shaped to govern the global economy. Manuel Castells, on the other hand, argues that the rise of the global network economy has given rise to diverse groupings of globally engaged capitalists, too fragmented to be conceptualized as a single coherent class (2000). Capital, he suggests, has escaped the control of any single class of people.

Seen in this light, the eagerness of Central American elites to embrace CAFTA despite its inclusion of intellectual property provisions that unambiguously disadvantage national industry appears less puzzling. Whether or not we conceptualize them as members of a single transnational class, it is clear that most of the region's pharmaceutical executives and trade negotiators are deeply embedded in transnational social, political, and economic circuits; they identify more with many residents of Miami or Houston than with the peasants of their country's hinterlands. The national state retains relevance under such a system—indeed, it is an essential piece for ensuring macroeconomic stability required for the functioning of the global capitalist system, as well as for ensuring some modicum of social order, particularly important given the disruptions engendered by the erosion of the social safety net. But it is less and less a meaningful forum for orchestrating politics in response to citizen demands and more a set of institutions placed at the service of transnational enterprise.[8]

This shifting role of the state has important implications for our state-centric regime of rights protection. The rise of intellectual property law in Central America casts in sharp relief the inadequacy of such a system, for the nation-states of Central America are not the architects of the abuse in question, and they have shown themselves incapable or unwilling of resisting those who are.[9] In Guatemala, for example, the Congress passed IP laws written by the U.S. embassy entirely in English, a language that only a slim fragment of the population speaks. In El Salvador, the laws were rammed through the legislature via emergency measures and a vote held in the middle of the night to preclude popular protest. And even in the United States, intellectual property policies are dictated by private industry more than democratic process.

Hardt and Negri describe a "new notion of right, or rather, a new inscription of authority and a new design of the production of norms and legal instruments of coercion that guarantee contracts and resolve conflicts. . . . The transition we are witnessing today is from traditional international law, which was defined by contracts and treaties, to the definition and constitution of a new sovereign, supranational world power" (Hardt and Negri 2000). The inscription, ever deeper, of Central American nation-states in legal systems operating largely beyond the reach of popular participation is a key step in this transition to global governance.

Why do these details matter? In classical liberal theory, the state's role is limited by citizens who would never agree to rules that disfavor their interests; a check on state power is provided by a rational populace. Yet, in today's world, it is increasingly apparent that many policies are decided by forces beyond the control of poor states; if anything, poor countries' states serve as a buffer to absorb protest while policies, dictated elsewhere, are pushed forward. This has profound implications for politics in the Global South. Not only Arendt's archetypal refugee but also indeed large swaths of the global population who reside in nations increasingly unable to resist their inscription into global legal systems that obligate them to take actions that advantage transnational capital over the bulk of their citizenry are effectively outside traditional mechanisms of human rights protection. Under what human rights convention is the U.S. trade representative obligated to refrain from violating the rights of Guatemalan AIDS patients? And in what court might they seek redress should she do so?

Rights and Biopolitics
There is a second significant way in which the advance of globalization as we know it exacerbates the shortcomings of the liberal rights model. Here,

too, my critique is not a new one. Liberal rights, as Marx reminds us in *On the Jewish Question*, are premised on an artificial separation (Marx and Lederer 1958). Civil and political rights make possible the fiction of a world in which humanity is left to tend to its own affairs in private life, unimpeded by state intrusions, yet each person is guaranteed to be treated as an equal in the public or political sphere—able to vote, express opinions freely, organize a political party, and then return to a life of grinding misery at the end of the day. The problem, as Marx notes, is that the grinding misery is not itself seen as a rights violation under liberal guarantees; the system thus conceals material inequalities under a veneer of political equality. Numerous feminist scholars have further expounded on the problems, for women, of cordoning off the "private" sphere in this way. Within the contemporary human rights movement, recent years have seen no less than a sea change in thinking about such matters: Efforts are underway to expand the scope of rights to include social and economic rights and to insist on active state intervention to stop abuses in the "private" sphere, such as domestic violence; these attempt to address this critique. But, again, these measures may not go far enough.

As Michel Foucault, Giorgio Agamben, and others have argued, the hallmark of contemporary power is its role in the production and regulation of life itself, or biopower. Power no longer pauses at the threshold of private life; it marks an ever-broader terrain for its own penetration, drawing its justification from the need to develop, educate, elucidate, nourish. As Foucault explains,

> Since the classical age the West has undergone a very profound transformation of these mechanisms of power . . . There has been a . . . shift in the right of death, or at least a tendency to align itself with the exigencies of a life-administering power and to define itself accordingly. This death that was based on the right of the sovereign is now manifested as simply the reverse of the right of the social body to ensure, maintain, or develop its life. Yet wars were never as bloody as they have been since the nineteenth century, and all things being equal, never before did regimes visit such holocausts on their own populations. But this formidable power of death—and this is perhaps what accounts for part of its force and the cynicism with which it has so greatly expanded its limits—now presents itself

as the counterpart of a power that exerts a positive influence on life, that endeavors to administer, optimize, and multiply it, subjecting it to precise controls and comprehensive regulations. Wars are no longer waged in the name of a sovereign who must be defended; they are waged on behalf of the existence of everyone; entire populations are mobilized for the purpose of wholesale slaughter in the name of life necessity: massacres have become vital. (Foucault 1978)

So too does it become necessary, in the name of prosperity and progress, to sign laws condemning the poor to lack medicines—lamentable, perhaps, but necessary for countries to "develop." As intellectual property reveals, this is the genius of biopower; it permeates false divisions between private and public, stepping in to regulate not only the content of that most private of human geographies—the mind itself—but plunging yet deeper into determining who lives and who dies,[10] all in the name of scientific advancement and the rule of law.

As Hardt and Negri explain, under Empire,

The activites of corporations are no longer defined by the imposition of abstract command and the organization of simple theft and unequal exchange. Rather, they directly structure and articulate territories and populations. They tend to make nation-states merely instruments to record the flows of the commodities, monies, and populations they set in motion. The transnational corporations directly distribute labor power over various markets, functionally allocate resources, and organize hierarchically the various sectors of world production. . . . There is nothing, no "naked life," no external standpoint, that can be posed outside this field permeated by money; nothing escapes money. (Hardt and Negri 2000, 31–32)

There is, therefore, no personal or national sovereignty untouched by trade law, no "natural" realm outside the law's intrusion. Yet rather than rendering the personal political in a way that might fuel resistance, the spread of biopower achieves the opposite: It renders politics personal, constraining the space for collective action by reducing the scope for opposition to only a few pitched battles, while meanwhile the inexorable spread of the system continues quietly apace.

It is difficult to imagine a more quintessential example of biopower than intellectual property. Yet such challenges map awkwardly onto the conventional regime of rights protection for a number of reasons. First, the inscription of biopower is done in the name of "rights" itself; it is legitimated in the language of production and protection; it is promoted through the culture of development, held out as the promise of prosperity for countries on the brink. "Shine a light on human rights," long a mantra of Amnesty International, assumes rights violations transpire in dark dungeons, where torturers, once exposed, will recoil to avoid condemnation; the organization's iconic candle reflects the same idea. Yet shining a light on intellectual property reveals only stacks of readily available legal memoranda. There is no single shameworthy act to be exposed; rather the obscure recalibration of social priorities through an endless series of technical procedures. Taken in isolation, each appears innocuous and mind-numbingly uninteresting. But, taken together, these provisions cement a logic of market sovereignty in health decision making. First the patent term is extended, under apparently reasonable conditions; then a technical training program is introduced to improve the functioning of patent offices; new protocols are elaborated to govern the use of test data in applications for marketing approval, thus clarifying the work of health and safety agencies; commissions are appointed to harmonize safety standards in accordance with international guidelines; a web portal is introduced to facilitate the Ministry of Economy's access to drug approval data; the text of regulations governing the importation of controlled substances is revised; provisions on patentability are revised under expert guidance . . . where, in this interminable sequence of ostensibly minor events, did sovereignty "die out slowly, like a sweet fire, small and alone"?[11]

"What's going to be the body count?" I was asked by an impatient journalist who interrupted my long-winded explanation of CAFTA's intellectual property chapter in 2005. Quantifiability counts: The politics of rights responds well to violations experienced by identifiable individuals and attributable to knowing, culpable actors. This is true both in the courts and on the streets. But the new IP regime won't dispatch lawyers to wrest pills from the clenched fists of individual patients who now take them. At most, the new system will very gradually make it more costly for states to procure the latest drugs for their populations, thus limiting the numbers that can be served or mandating their treatment with older technologies. To discern an individual "victim" is difficult; what dies here is the vision of medicine as social, health as public, solidarity as laudatory. Liberal rights, and the politics of public denunciation we have devised to defend them, are at a disadvantage in countering such surreptitious offenses.

Indeed, Agamben asserts that abuses under the intellectual property regime are not simply undeterred by the scheme of rights but made possible by it:

> Declarations of rights represent the originary figure of the inscription of natural life in the juridico-political order of the nation-state. The same bare life that in the *ancien régime* was politically neutral and belonged to God as creaturely life and in the classical world was (at least apparently) clearly distinguished as *zoē* from political life (*bios*) now fully enters into the structure of the state and even becomes the earthly foundation of the state's legitimacy and sovereignty. (Agamben 1998)

Humanitarian organizations, therefore, traffic in images of bare or sacred life—the nameless orphan with the wide eyes and penetrating gaze—yet operate in "symmetry with state power" (133), producing a humanitarianism devoid of politics and ultimately incapable of disarming the power that causes the problem.

Where Are We Headed? Concluding Thoughts on the Emancipatory Potential of Rights

Lessons from the Central American IP struggles suggest that our tendency to speak about human rights as if the term referred to a single, recognized set of concepts or practices—and then arguing that that set is either inherently liberatory or inherently limiting—is part of the problem. There is not one single vision of "human rights" that gets altered or diluted when it hits the ground in concrete contexts. There are multiple visions, competing concepts. Some campaigns never launch; some ideas flare bright like a shooting star in the night sky, yet prove themselves equally evanescent; other conceptions, the workhorses of the field, have withstood decades of funding crises, critical challenges, and leadership transitions. Rather than asking whether rights "are" or "are not" liberatory in the context of injustices inscribed in the rules of the global economy, we should ask under what conditions efforts to promote rights come closest to that counter-hegemonic potential, and what constrains their ability to do so.

In this context, I believe the lessons from the Central American struggles over intellectual property should sharpen our thinking about human rights in two fundamental ways: how rights struggles are framed, and how different actors within transnational networks relate to one another. Both of them draw on an analysis of power.

Framing of Rights Struggles

First, the lessons from Central America suggest the need for greater attention to the way struggles are framed—to how we know what it is we're fighting for, anyway, and who decides.

These questions about framing have always been important; we know from existing scholarship that not all issues are equally suited for success through transnational advocacy mechanisms. Keck and Sikkink suggest that "causes that can be assigned to the deliberate actions of identifiable individuals" are more likely to be successful, as are "issues involving bodily harm to vulnerable individuals, especially where there is a short and clear causal chain assigning responsibility" (1998, 27). For this reason, undoubtedly, anti-IP activists feel pressed to describe their struggle in simple, evocative terms; when forced to elaborate detailed, technical descriptions of test data exclusivity and its perils, the power of their narrative breaks down.

Yet there may be ways in which rendering the complex issue simple also limits its transformative potential. As I argue in Chapter 3, even advocates of the so-called counterhegemonic vision of health rights in IP struggles often pitch their arguments on highly questionable terrain. Ultimately, their opposition to intellectual property rights rests on the premise that monopolies limit competition in the market, that competition favors lower prices, and that lower prices are preferable for consumers, especially poor ones. Yet concealed within this argument is an unacknowledged concession that market rules should play a determinative role in health decision making.

In arguing stridently for more competition to lower prices,[12] we are not asking more fundamental questions about the wisdom of marketizing social life, even its most sacred corners. Accepting market logic leaves uncomplicated certain assumptions about the virtues of competition and of the generics industry in particular, which some inconvenient evidence suggests may not be true. What's more, such campaigns let the state off easy, for although exorbitant prices undoubtedly impose additional burdens, even a cursory look at state pharmaceutical decision making in Central America calls into question whether states are complying with their basic human rights obligations to begin with—even without the additional pressures of intellectual property.

Chapter 5 also underscores the perils of misreading rights. While the cascade of individual rights claims upheld by the Guatemalan courts may indeed have provided drugs to patients whose lives depend on them, the way in which the court's judgments interlock with intellectual property rules to promote commercial monopolies should give us pause. In these cases, the two aforementioned critiques of rights are evident: Rights enforcement is historically primed to see violations in individual terms and to cast the state as the primary culprit. Yet in a world where rights are the last discourse standing, what of solidarity or sustainability as the basis for social policy?

The question is not so much whether *rights* are counterhegemonic but whether this rendering of them is. Can we imagine alternative rights-based discourses? Who decides which ones triumph and which founder?

More recent research on the framing of rights campaigns offers some clues in this regard. Carpenter (2007), for example, insists on the importance of not only understanding which campaigns win but also of looking for the "dogs that don't bark"—the potential campaigns that were never launched. Her research shows that certain nodes in the network function as "gatekeepers" and that their decisions about which issues get taken up respond as much to perceptions of political space or internetwork relationships as they do to the inherent right or wrong of a given practice. Similarly, Lake and Wong's study of issue emergence highlights the central role of organizations like Amnesty International in determining which issues receive the attention of the human rights movement as a whole (2009). In other words, transnational advocacy networks don't simply tap into sui generis rights concerns but in many cases create issues out of whole cloth, and not all parties are equally endowed with the ability to shape such decision making. In intellectual property, this becomes a fundamental question: Who decides these matters, and why?

Power and Relations within Advocacy Networks

Recent work undertaken by Sally Merry and a range of collaborators has shed important light on how issues, once adopted by a network, get translated across space and time by key participants. This work has been particularly important in calling attention to the pivotal role played by local interlocutors—translators, to use Merry's 2005 terminology—who actively repackage global rights concepts in terms that make sense in the context and culture of the countries in which they operate and vice versa. This fine grain focus on the "how" of network operations allows us to sidestep some of the more black-and-white thinking that characterizes work on human rights by both advocates and detractors, particularly the frequent notion that rights are a Northern imposition on poor countries. Indeed, Merry and her collaborators make great strides in showing how rights concepts are rendered malleable in the hands of Southern Hemisphere actors, whose role is one of active transformation at every turn.

Yet even Merry and her colleagues retain some assumptions about how rights work that would benefit from further examination. As argued in Chapter 4, progressive Central American health activists have historically focused on improving the quality and accessibility of state health services, still the primary impediment to the enjoyment of health in the region; they have made such arguments while invoking domestic and international referents to the concept of health as a human right. While some observers might read Central Americans' limited uptake of IP as evidence of a lack of capacity on an intensely technical issue—and not wrongly, as the barriers to entry in this field are formidable—I argue that it speaks more to a mismatch between the way Central American health activists understood right-to-health struggles and the way in which it was framed by transnational campaigners.

Many of these assumptions are inescapable in what David Engel has called the "vertical perspective" on transnational legalism, an approach that "traces concepts or practices from what are conceived as higher, more powerful, prestigious or inclusive levels of legal organization to what are conceived as lower, less powerful, more localized levels" (Engel 2012). Such studies tend to assume that societies in the South receive human rights ideas like packages from the North and that any variations evident in Southern renderings of rights are the result of their distortion throughout this translation process. Engel's point is that rights are not the only game in town; other discursive frameworks are far more frequently invoked by his research subjects in Thailand and may indeed may be more meaningful and transformative for them, but the vertical emphasis on rights' travel "up and down" international networks fails to capture what other ideas may be in circulation horizontally.

My argument here does not rest on the effort to capture shared frameworks of meaning "outside rights" for understanding disputes or challenging events. Rather, I argue that there may often be multiple rights discourses available, rather than just one. And therefore the assumption that international or transnational actors are somehow best positioned to discern the rights approach and to transmit it to their local interlocutors for application "on the ground" becomes problematic. Merry and her co-authors insist that it is the connection to the universal that renders rights "magic"; indeed, other scholars have commented on the way that framing a local conflict in rights terms "verticalizes" the issue, vaunting it beyond the local and making available a range of allies to advocate for its solution. Clearly, some connection to broader conceptions of justice must take place for any struggle to become known beyond the immediate geographic locality in which it unfolds and hence for international allies to become involved, tipping the balance in favor of those actors who might otherwise be marginalized or ignored. Yet why do we assume that those actors situated closest to the transnational level are uniquely well positioned to connect rights struggles in faraway lands to international agreements?

Bursting the Binaries
"Free" trade versus human rights?
My overall point in this book is not to criticize the specific decisions made by those leading the access to medicines movement or to condemn anyone's effort to tap market mechanisms for social good. Nor is it to banish drug producers, generic or originator, from discussions of social policy. Rather, my point is to ask what is gained and lost by pitching our battles

on such terrain. When we imagine the battle for public health as a quest to unleash the market, are we surrendering before we start in that ultimate struggle to construct a society guided by principles of solidarity rather than economic growth? Oddly, we have arrived at a point where the corporate wolves of free trade cloak themselves in the sheep's clothing of human rights, and vice versa: Human rights advocates pitch their arguments in the language of free trade! In such a contest, the space for maneuver is so reduced as to make the discourses redundant.

North versus South?

If this book complicates the assumed contradiction between "free" trade and human rights, it also underscores the need to question other familiar binaries, in particular the North/South binaries so common in discussions of trade justice. This is important for at least two reasons: first, because, as others have observed, such labels obscure the vast diversity within each category. In the field of intellectual property, this is particularly important: Studies of the "Global South" based on Brazil or India have produced policy proposals that transnational activists sought to promote during the battles over CAFTA. Yet vast differences separate Hyderabad from Honduras, and "one size fits all" strategies for Global South resistance failed in Central America. This has practical, empirical dimensions: As discussed in Chapter 2, in Central America test data protection is a far more frequently relevant form of IP than patents; yet, if we were to derive our sense of what matters across the Global South from the experience of Brazil or India, we would devote principal attention to patents alone and miss this. Of course, this has tactical implications, too; as discussed in Chapter 4, in Central America right to health struggles have focused on boosting state capacity to perform such vital functions as regulating the safety of the drug supply. Until states assume some basic responsibilities such as these, battles against transnational targets like Big Pharma may resonate poorly with local priorities.

But, second, in this context of extraordinarily illegitimate institutions, rights practices are particularly prone to antistate pitfalls, as argued in Chapter 5. If Brazil and India are "Global South" countries, they sure look Northern in comparison to El Salvador and Guatemala. Ultimately, I suggest, as human rights advocates increasingly tackle challenges on economic terrain, we cannot afford to forget that markets become relevant to human welfare only via their embeddedness in social institutions, including especially the state. Not all states engage with markets equally, and not all forms of engagement produce equal results. A call for trade justice that grounds itself in market access alone, or that allocates countries to "North" or "South" categories without a more nuanced analysis of their behavior, misses these important distinctions between societies and ultimately fails to ensure benefits to those who are most vulnerable.

Transnational versus local?

What's more, as scholars of human rights we play an important role in understanding and legitimating rights campaigns—and yet too often the frameworks we use for understanding rights embed a related binary between the local and the transnational, linked by a presumed vertical relationship. This language of verticality is so enmeshed in our thinking that it becomes difficult to talk about human rights without invoking it: Even in these pages, I describe the struggles over rights in Central America as unfolding "on the ground," as if this existed in opposition to discussions over rights unfolding in some ethereal, extraterritorial space at the transnational level! Such conceptual categories come dangerously close to confining "local" actors to a place of secondary importance as receivers, rather than architects, of rights—presumed to be a preexisting package of ideas, passed on by transnational advocates.

Yet, in my research in Central America, this binary simply doesn't hold. I spoke to actors from a range of sectors, but each of them was deeply enmeshed in transnational communities that shaped their approach to rights, health, and politics. Members of patients' rights groups spoke about their attendance at international conferences and offered to put me in touch with counterpart organizations in other Latin American countries. Pharmaceutical executives—whether from Big or Little Pharma—talked about their relationships to global markets, both as sources for raw materials and targets for their finished product. State officials described international trade agreements and their intersections with domestic law as the opportunities and constraints within which their work unfolded. Health activists invoked the leading theoreticians and practitioners of the social medicine movement or mentioned workshops or trainings attended abroad. Access to medicines advocates, too, were unmistakably enmeshed in global networks that helped frame their understanding of the issues at stake. So what, then, distinguishes the "local" from the "transnational"? My point here is not that distinctions do not exist; a core argument of this book is that something substantial separates the way those in Guatemala City and Geneva viewed this issue during the period under study. Nor is my point to argue that one node is more "right" than another; clearly, for human rights tactics to work, we need all links in the chain to operate coherently. A struggle that doesn't transcend the particulars of Guatemala City is one in which locally powerful elites will almost always win, just as a struggle conceived in Geneva without connection to Guatemalan realities will undoubtedly prove ineffective.

However, it seems important to note that what distinguishes "transnational" from "local" may be more about access to power and resources than about epistemological clarity. Ultimately, it's not the magic of universality but the connections and credibility of international campaigners—the likelihood that the *New York Times* will call them for the "body count" and ascribe some credence to the answer they give—that can tip the scales for justice in a conflict that might otherwise remain strictly localized. Geneva- or New York-based human rights organizations enjoy access to powerful governments, media, technology, and specialized training that may be difficult or impossible for Central American activists to obtain on their own. The role of advocates who work in Northern institutions, then, is fundamental in making rights work but not because, by virtue of some presumed greater proximity to the international realm, they are best situated to formulate what rights should mean.

Perhaps the best way to conceive of relationships in advocacy networks would be more pluralistic; rather than a single axis of struggle on which rights packages slide "up" and "down," we should imagine the transformative site as the place whereby differently situated actors might come together behind shared understandings of what is worth fighting for. Rather than the downward application of predefined rights, the advocacy network's task is the construction of new imaginings. The more diverse our understandings of rights can be, the greater counterhegemonic potential they can admit. But for us to notice this when it happens, we need to burst forth from the binaries that have confined our thinking for so long.

Conclusion

In these pages I have argued that human rights and free trade may come into contradiction on matters of intellectual property and that the debates represent a struggle for hegemony between two competing discourses, two sets of rules by which globalization is to be conducted. But the ultimate importance of that contradiction is lost if both contenders' arguments pivot on the axis of market rule. If human rights is to offer a potentially transformative way of understanding our world, its advocates need to recognize that intellectual property law is more than the sum of its parts—it is more than simply a roster of regulations to govern drugs' entrance to markets. It is the latest in a series of waves that have swept the continent, substituting markets for values, efficiency for justice. As Agamben writes, "Nothing is more dismal than this unconditional being-in-force of juridical categories in a world in which they no longer mirror any comprehensive ethical content" (cited in Douzinas 2007, 126). If in the name of human rights we argue only over whether test data protection should be conferred for five or fifteen years, without perceiving the deeper effects of intellectual property policy on the logic underlying our world or equipping our activists with tools to resist them, we will have lost even when we win.

Yet there remains the possibility of another outcome. There is not one unitary "human rights" but a diversity of conceptions and practices. Ultimately, if human rights is to be a vehicle for counterhegemony in today's world, we need to resuscitate alternative imaginings of what the word *rights* means. This is not a call for a new paradigm; it is a call for greater attention to the diversity often muffled within the existing paradigm and particularly to the voices and imaginings of actors from the front lines of access struggles around the globe, who might yet point us in directions that push forward the rights paradigm in truly transformative ways.

Reference Matter

Notes

Chapter 1

1. Latter-day agreements' relatively more relaxed standards are the result of a shift in U.S. trade policies following the congressional elections of 2006, which led to the adoption of the New Trade Policy for America. However, there are some specific provisions in later agreements that exceed those in CAFTA; my argument here isn't that CAFTA is toughest on every possible dimension, only that taken together its provisions are the most demanding.

Chapter 2

1. Valerio sustained, unconvincingly in my view, that the Central Americans had successfully resisted U.S. pressures to make CAFTA a TRIPS-plus agreement.

2. As Robert Kuttner explains, "To be a liberal internationalist meant that one supported republican political institutions and laissez-faire economics at home, free flows of capital and goods across national frontiers, and a hopeful, irenic sense of world community" (Kuttner 1991); "America's liberal internationalists saw their mission as projecting U.S. power into the world—but in order to teach universal virtues, not to pursue narrow nationalistic goals. . . . This universalist internationalism invariably went hand-in-hand with laissez-faire economics" (1991: 32).

3. It is not entirely a departure from past practice, as human rights appeals have almost always demanded that states take positive actions to uphold rights, not simply refrain from violating them in the first place; these have historically included such things as carrying out investigations into past violations and punishing those responsible, or designing new policies to avert future abuses. But such appeals typically had secondary or tertiary importance in campaigns designed to rein in offending states; today's campaigns, more and more, ask states to take a proactive role in the promotion of human rights.

4. This is very significant, for although lax protections for labor and the environment could arguably serve as "floors" for later improvements as countries' economies develop, it is much more difficult to imagine stringent IP protections

as a first step toward economic growth, let alone the fulfillment of broader social goals, in the Global South.

Chapter 3

1. Guatemala is, as it turns out, an attractive site for drugmakers looking to conduct clinical trials. As the website of one company aiming to build relationships with the pharmaceutical researchers crows,

> Guatemala is among the worst performers in terms of health outcomes in Latin America, with one of the highest infant mortality rates, and one of the lowest life expectancies at birth. Yet, like many countries of Latin America, Guatemala is in a stage of epidemiologic transition from infectious to chronic diseases as major sources of morbidity and mortality . . . Guatemala has a large drug and treatment naïve population due to the lack of available medical care. These factors make it an ideal environment for many types of drug and device clinical trials. (Americas Clinical)

2. As of this writing, however, the health system in El Salvador is in the midst of important reforms aiming to address this problem by integrating the disparate branches into a single health system.

3. In recent years, Central American governments have also begun a collaborative process of joint purchasing for a few drugs, as a way to lowering prices through economies of scale; this process is still incipient.

4. Recognizing the importance of informing national implementation processes, UNCTAD (UN Conference on Trade and Development) and ICTSD (International Centre for Trade and Sustainable Development) commissioned a dialogue with Argentine IP expert Carlos Correa in which he instructed Central American countries how to implement test data protection to conform with CAFTA's requirements while preserving as much latitude as possible for public health considerations. To guide these discussions, Correa drafted a "Model Law" for CAFTA implementation (Correa 2006a).

5. Or, alternately, some studies conclude by demonstrating that IP-protected drugs are more expensive than different drugs in the same therapeutic class for which there is competition. For example, Shaffer and Brenner make such an argument about Guatemala (see note 54). Here, again, the assumption is that were IP protection not producing a monopoly, healthy competition would drive down prices so that they might resemble the prices of other drugs in the class. This may indeed be the case, but it relies on the assumption that, absent IP, the market would produce competition. My point here is that we should make sure this is truly the case because markets are not always or "naturally" competitive.

6. This is an argument I myself have made on multiple occasions, particularly because it is an easy way to achieve political traction—it's essentially a "free trade" argument—so I am as guilty as anyone else of this practice.

7. For example, in the U.S. market, at least two studies have shown an inverse relationship between the number of drugs competing in the market and the average price; see Congressional Budget Office, 1998; and Caves, et al.,1991). But the number of competing drugs matters: see Frank and Salkever, 1997. As Reiffen and Ward write, "Generic drug prices fall with increasing number of competitors but remain above long-run marginal cost until there are 8 or more competitors" (Reiffen and Ward, 2006).

8. Full disclosure: I lack evidence to support this assertion that branded drugs are safer; although many physicians in Central America share this assumption, I'm not aware of any studies that prove this to be true. The government is equally ineffective at monitoring the integrity of branded drugs. However, one might assume that companies investing in branding strategies—whether for originator or generic drugs—have an economic incentive to reduce the risk of negative publicity associated with their brand and therefore would implement more rigorous internal quality controls. Companies selling a product whose primary competitive feature is its low price may not share such incentives.

9. An exact translation of this term does not exist in English, nor does a precise equivalent exist in the U.S. legal system. In practice the amparo is similar to an injunction; when granted it mandates an immediate halt to an activity deemed threatening to fundamental rights.

10. Brazil announced its intention use a compulsory license for Kaletra in 2005 but eventually reached an agreement in negotiations with Abbott, thus averting the issuing of the license. Thailand issued a compulsory license for Kaletra in 2007, prompting immediate retaliation from Abbott, who declared it would withhold seven new drugs it had previously planned to introduce to the Thai market. More recently, civil society groups in Colombia have campaigned (unsuccessfully) to convince their government to issue a compulsory license for Kaletra.

11. Shaffer and Brenner, for example, largely rely on the assertions of generics manufacturers in Guatemala to measure CAFTA's impact. While certainly generics producers are valuable interlocutors on this issue, they should not be taken as a stand-in for public health groups.

12. It is difficult to know exactly how much money has been spent, as direct purchasing prices are not publicly divulged. Yet a rough estimate of Kaletra spending might assume the following: According to publicly available data, the government planned to purchase 2,307,600 tablets of Kaletra in 2009. In the last year for which pricing data was available, 2005, the government purchased this drug for 20.255 quetzales per pill (in the 133/33 concentration). Assuming the same price, and multiplying it by the projected purchase for 2009, produces a total of almost US$6 million at current exchange rates, to treat approximately 1,060 patients, for a per-patient annual cost of $5,500.

Chapter 4

1. Román Macaya, for example, suggested that if the study had looked at 2001 instead of 2003, the case of antiretroviral Nelfinavir, which the Caja obtained in generic form that year, would illustrate the dangers of data exclusivity. That drug was first registered on the Costa Rican market in 1997, and, if data exclusivity had been applicable in 2001, a generic version would not have been available until 2002.

Chapter 5

1. In El Salvador, barriers to access remain high for everyday citizens seeking medications. Although the country gave rise to the landmark case of *Jorge Odir Miranda et al v. El Salvador*, in which the Inter-American Commission ordered the provision of antiretroviral drugs to HIV patients, it has not seen a subsequent wave of similar cases and will therefore not be addressed in this chapter.

2. An exact translation does not exist in English. Sometimes translated as writ of amparo, in fact the term *amparo* refers to the entire judicial proceeding, more than simply the writ. In practice the amparo, when granted, functions something like an injunction, mandating immediate cessation of the activity that is deemed threatening.

3. In Colombia, the amparo is known as a *tutela*.

4. At present, only decisions from cases that reach the Constitutional Court are publicly available. Under Guatemala's system, other courts may hear constitutional cases, though the Constitutional Court retains sole authority on appeal. Informants told me that the overwhelming majority of access to medicines cases brought before lower courts were appealed to the Constitutional Court, but any that were not are excluded from analysis here. And within the cases in the court's online database, access is imperfect due to the way the database is organized and the suboptimal functionality of its search function.

5. These cases arise because of IGSS policies stipulating that affiliated patients who are not employed due to their medical condition can be granted treatment while on medical leave from employment for a period of up to fifty-two weeks, at which time they must solicit a new status as disabled pensioner (*pensión por invalidez*) or risk termination of coverage. Some patients either failed to complete the paperwork to make this transition or found that IGSS had failed to process their request, and coverage was therefore terminated in semiarbitrary fashion. Similarly, per IGSS rules, children are covered under their parents' eligibility up to age fifteen; in some cases, children with chronic conditions found their treatment abruptly suspended because of their age and appealed to the courts for relief.

6. Other sources also confirm diarrhea and nausea as frequent, if avoidable, side effects of Cellcept; see, for example, the American College of Rheumatology's information sheet "Mycophenolate Mofetil (CellCept)and Mycophenolate Sodium (Myfortic)," available at www.rheumatology.org/practice/clinical/patients/.../mycophenolate.p.... (retrieved on January 3, 2013).

Chapter 6

1. In the interests of accuracy and fairness to Greg Grandin: In Grandin 2005, his critique is primarily aimed at the work of truth commissions, not human rights writ large, but I believe that to some degree it can be extended to human rights campaigns targeting particular repressive regimes and framing them as departures from the established norm.

2. As David Kennedy charges, "The human rights movement suggests that 'rights,' rather than people taking political decisions, can bring emancipation. This demobilizes other actors and other vocabularies, and encourages emancipation through reliance on enlightened, professional elites with 'knowledge' of rights and wrongs, alienating people from themselves and from the vocabulary of their own governance" (2004, 22).

3. Grandin's critique suggests that this term is in fact a misnomer, as the post–Cold War "democracies" that dot the region differ greatly from their prewar antecedents. The principal difference lies in their adoption of individual rights models that more closely resemble U.S. liberal conceptions, unlike the constitutions grounded in social rights that characterized earlier regimes.

4. Here I am referring to the hallmark tactics of Amnesty International and other organizations who direct appeals to governments on behalf of those whose rights are violated. Of course, these classic campaigns often feature more than letter writing and can include more complex forms of intergovernmental lobbying, legal cases, media work, and other components. I simplify here for the sake of readability only.

5. This is most obviously true in the cases where European powers seek to hold tyrants of other nations accountable in their domestic courts (a la Pinochet). The International Criminal Court, while substantially weakened by the opposition of the United States, comes closer to remedying this problem.

6. Of course, the liberation of labor is partial and, from a human rights point of view, problematic: Economic forces encourage migration across borders, yet political forces root rights-protection in the states of origin, so growing numbers of migrant laborers are effectively outside the reach of labor law by virtue of their undocumented status in the country where they work.

7. As Robinson explains, "In sum, a global class structure is becoming superimposed on national class structures. As national productive structures become transnationally integrated, world classes whose organic development took place through the nation-state are experiencing supranational integration with 'national' classes of other countries. This global class formation involves the increasing division of the world into a global bourgeoisie and a global proletariat, even though global labor remains highly stratified along old and new social hierarchies that cut across national boundaries." (2004: 43)

8. This is not inherently and always the case, as one can imagine states where dissident factions uncommitted, or even opposed, to implementing the

"Washington Consensus," have captured power (Venezuela, Bolivia, and Ecuador come to mind . . .). But it is certainly the case throughout the small countries of Central America, who enjoy few advantages in resisting transnational capitalist hegemony.

9. Of course, the imposition of U.S. policies on Central American populaces is not new; yet today's system differs from old-style imperialism in significant ways. As William Robinson (1996) has explained, U.S. foreign policy has shifted from the installing of friendly dictators to the promotion of something resembling "democracy"—yet gutted of true transformative potential. The logic by which these policies are promoted is not the raw power of the U.S. military—though military intervention remains a powerful disincentive to noncompliance, the possibility of which is always present—but rather the more seductive promises of development, economic growth, and the rule of law. The result of these processes is a local law written to serve transnational interests; CAFTA mandates this, in the name of freedom.

10. In a world in which approximately four people die of AIDS per minute (UNAIDS 2007), and yet new medicines available to those who can afford them allow the management of this disease as a chronic affliction, deciding who has access to medicines *is the same thing as* deciding who lives and who dies.

11. This line is taken from Guatemalan poet Otto René Castillo's "Intelectuales apolíticos."

12. The debates over intellectual property and access to medicines reveal this tendency to praise purported solutions precisely because they engage the market. For example, in a recent op-ed piece rebutting Pharma's arguments on the value of patents, Robert Weissman, director of Essential Action, argues, "Rather than criticizing countries like Thailand that are issuing lawful compulsory licenses—government authorizations of generic competition for products that remain on patent—Mr. Ayodele should be pointing to them as an example to be followed. They are, after all, promoting market competition and lowering price" (Weissman 2008).

References

Agamben, Giorgio. 1998. *Homo sacer. sovereign power and bare life.* Stanford, CA: Stanford University Press.

Almeida, Paul. 2010. El Salvador: Elecciones y movimientos sociales. *Revista De Ciencia Política (Santiago)* 30 (2): 319. Retrieved on July 31, 2011, from www .scielo.cl/scielo.php?pid=S0718-090X2010000200008&script=sci_arttext.

Americas Clinical. Guatemala and Latin America: Building strong relationships. In Americas Clinical [database online]. Retrieved on July 27, 2011, from www.americasclinical.com/guatemala-latin-america/.

Anderson, Robert D., and Hannu Wager. 2006. Human rights, development, and the WTO: The cases of intellectual property and competition policy. *Journal of International Economic Law* 9 (3) (September): 707–747.

Angell, Marcia. 2004. *The truth about the drug companies: How they deceive us and what to do about it.* New York: Random House.

Archila, E. J., G. Carrasquilla, M. Melendez, and J. P. Uribe. 2005. *Estudio sobre la propiedad intelectual en el sector farmaceutico colombiano.* Bogota: Fedesarrollo, Fundación para la Educación Superior y el Desarrollo e Fundación Santa Fé.

Asamblea Legislativa de la República de Costa Rica. *Ley de informacion no Divulgada*, Public Law 7975, (2000). Retrieved on July 29, 2011, from http://ministeriopublico.poder-judicial.go.cr/coop-intern/Normativa%20Nacional/10-Propiedad%20Intelectual/08.pdf.

Attaran, Amir, and Lee Gillespie-White. 2001. Do patents for antiretroviral drugs constrain access to AIDS treatment in Africa? *JAMA: The Journal of the American Medical Association* 286 (15) (October 17): 1886–1892.

Barrett, Ann, Tom Roques, Matthew Small, and Richard D. Smith. 2006. How much will herceptin really cost? *BMJ* 333 (7578) (November 25): 1118–1120.

Bogo, Jorge. 2007. *Análisis desde el punto de vista de la defensa de la competencia de los mercados de medicamentos para el tratamiento de las enfermedades cardiovasculares, respiratorias y gastrointestinales en el salvador. informe de resultados.* San Salvador: Superintendencia de Competencia, República de El Salvador. Retrieved on July 30, 2011, from www.sc.gob.sv/pages .php?Id=206.

Boyle, James. 2008. *The public domain: Enclosing the commons of the mind.* New Haven, CT, and London: Yale University Press.

Burton, Bob, and Andy Rowell. 2003. From patient activism to Astroturf marketing. *PR Watch (Published by the Center for Media and Democracy)* 10 (1) (2003). Retrieved on September 15, 2011, from www.prwatch.org/epublish/1/32.

Carpenter, R. Charli. 2007. Setting the advocacy agenda: Theorizing issue emergence and nonemergence in transnational advocacy networks. *International Studies Quarterly* 51, 99–120.

Castells, Manuel. 2000. The rise of the network society: The information age: Economy, society, and culture, volume 1, 2nd ed. Malden, MA, and Oxford, UK: Blackwell.

Caves, R. E., M. E. Whinston, and M. A. Hurwitz. 1991. "Patent expiration, entry, and competition in the US pharmaceutical industry: an exploratory analysis," *Brookings Papers on Economic Activity: Microeconomics.* Washington, DC: Brookings Institute, 1–66.

Center for Pharmaceutical Management. 2003. *Access to essential medicines: El Salvador. 2001.* Arlington, VA: Management Sciences for Health.

Centro de Investigaciones Económicas Nacionales (CIEN). 2006. *Economía informal: Superando las barreras de un estado excluyente.* Guatemala City: CIEN.

Cerón, Alejandro, and Angelina Snodgrass Godoy. 2009. Intellectual property and access to medicines: An analysis of legislation in Central America. *Bulletin of the World Health Organization* 87 (1): 787.

Chaves, Gabriela Costa, and Maria Auxiliadora Oliveira. 2007. A proposal for measuring the degree of public health–sensitivity of patent legislation in the context of the WTO TRIPS agreement. *Bulletin of the World Health Organization* 85 (1): 49.

Coalicion por la Transparencia. 2005. *Informe de analisis del proceso para adquisicion de medicamentos para las instituciones del sector de salud pública en guatemala.* Guatemala City: Coalicion por la Transparencia.

Congreso de la República de Guatemala. 2005. *Decreto 30-2005: Reformas a la Ley de Propiedad Industrial.* Retrieved on January 4, 2013, from www.oj.gob .gt/es/.../decretos/D030-2005.pdf.

———. *Decreto 9-2003*, (2003). *Reforma a la ley de propiedad industrial*. Retrieved on July 26, 2011, from www.sgp.gob.gt/PaginaWeb/Decretos%202003/DG9-2003.pdf.

———. *Decreto 34-2004*. (2004). *Reformas a la ley de propiedad industrial, Decreto no. 57-2000*. Retrieved on July 26, 2011, from www.oj.gob.gt/es/QueEsOJ/EstructuraOJ/UnidadesAdministrativas/CentroAnalisisDocumentacion Judicial/cds/CDs%20leyes/2004/PDFs/Decretos/DECRETO%2034-04.pdf; published as *Acuerdo 6-2003* (2003a).

———. *Decreto 30-2005*, (2005). Retrieved on July 28, 2011, from www.lexdelta.com/cutrigua/ficha_ley_cutrigua.php?numerol=4457&codigo=DC30-2005.

Congressional Budget Office, *How Increased Competition from Generic Drugs Has Affected Prices and Returns in the Pharmaceutical Industry* (Washington, DC: CBO, 1998).

Connolly, Ceci. 2005. Pentagon to drop Nexium from its list of covered drugs for military personnel; 'purple pill' Nexium the first to be cut. *The Washington Post*, May 8. Available at http://search.proquest.com/docview/409830994? accountid=14784.

Consejo Centroamericano de Protección al Consumidor, CONCADECO. 2008. *Sondeo de precios de medicamentos centroamericano*. San José, Costa Rica: CONCADECO.

ConSuAccion (Consumidores en Acción de Centroamérica). 2007. *Promoción etica y precio justo en los medicamentos? una mirada desde las organizaciones de consumidores en centroamérica*. San Salvador: ConSuAcción (Consumidores en Acción de Centroamérica),

Correa, Carlos. 2006a. *Implementación de la protección de datos de prueba de productos farmacéuticos y agroquímicos en DR-CAFTA-ley modelo*. Geneva: International Centre for Trade and Sustainable Development (ICTSD).

———. 2006b. Implications of bilateral free trade agreements on access to medicines. *Bulletin of the World Health Organization* 84 (5): 399.

Corte de Constitucionalidad de Guatemala. 2008. Apelación de sentencia de amparo, expediente 1600-2008. In *Corte de Constitucionalidad de la República de Guatemala*. Retrieved on October 21, 2011, from www.cc.gob.gt/siged2009/mdlConsultas/frmVerDocumento.aspx?St_DocumentoId= 804532.html&St_RegistrarConsulta=yes.

Davis, Jeffrey, and Edward H. Warner. 2007. Reaching beyond the state: Judicial independence, the inter-American court of human rights, and accountability in Guatemala. *Journal of Human Rights* 6 (2) (04): 233–255. Available at http:// search.ebscohost.com/login.aspx?direct=true&db=a9h&AN=25729270& site=ehost-live.

Deere, Carolyn. 2009. *The Implementation Game: The TRIPS agreement and the global politics of intellectual property reform in developing countries.* Oxford, UK: Oxford University Press.

Dezalay, Yves, and Bryant G. Garth. 2006. Human rights from the Cold War to Kosovo: The rise and renewal of international human rights as a socio-legal field. *Annual Review of Law and Social Science* 2: 231–255.

Dirección Normativa de Contrataciones y Adquisiciones del Estado. (2008). Listado de especificaciones DNCAE no. 14-2008 in Direccion Normativa de Contrataciones y Adquisiciones del Estado [database online]. Retrieved on July 30, 2011, from www.guatecompras.gt/concursos/files/158/788791@Listado%20Especificaciones%20DNCAE%2014-2008.pdf.

Doctors Without Borders. 2012, July. Untangling the web of antiretroviral price reductions, 15th ed. Retrieved on July 27, 2012, from http://utw.msfaccess.org.

Donahue, John M. 1989. International organizations, health services, and nation building in Nicaragua. *Medical Anthropology Quarterly* 3 (3, The Political Economy of Primary Health Care in Costa Rica, Guatemala, Nicaragua, and El Salvador) (September): 258–269. Available at www.jstor.org/stable/648642.

Douzinas, Costas. 2007. *Human rights and empire: The political philosophy of cosmopolitanism.* London and New York: Routledge-Cavendish.

Drahos, Peter. 1997. Thinking strategically about intellectual property rights. *Telecommunications Policy* 21 (3) (4): 201–211.

———. 2007. Four lessons for developing countries from the trade negotiations over access to medicines. *Liverpool Law Review* 28:11.

Drahos, Peter, and John Braithwaite. 2003. *Information feudalism: Who owns the knowledge economy?* London: The New Press.

Dyer, Geoff. 2003. Debate is raging over whether Nexium, a widely used ulcer drug, is really a worthwhile improvement for most patients over an earlier treatment—especially with healthcare budgets under growing pressure, writes Geoff Dyer. *Financial Times*, Oct 22. Available at http://search.proquest.com/docview/249442739?accountid=14784.

Engel, David. 2012. "Vertical and Horizontal Perspectives on Rights Consciousness," *Indiana Journal of Global Legal Studies*, 19, 423–455.

Espinoza Fiallos, Eduardo, and Giovanni Guevara. 2007. *Disponibilidad y precio de los medicamentos en el salvador durante el segundo semestre de 2006.* San Salvador: Universidad de El Salvador.

Espinoza Fiallos, Eduardo, Maria Angela Marroquín Elías, and Giovanni Guevara. 2009. *Caracterización del Sector Farmacéutico Nacional. El Salvador 2009.* San

Salvador: Observatorio de Políticas Públicas y Salud, Universidad de El Salvador. Retrieved on July 31, 2011, from www2.paho.org/hq/dmdocuments/2010/Informe%20Final%20de%20Resultados%20Investigacion%20Sector%20Farmaceutico.pdf.

Ferraz, O. 2009. The right to health in the courts of Brazil: Worsening health inequities? *Health and Human Rights: An International Journal* 11 (2). Available at www.hhrjournal.org/index.php/hhr/article/view/172/270.

Fiedler, John L. 1985. Latin American health policy and additive reform: The case of Guatemala. *International Journal of Health Services* 15 (2): 275.

Fishman, Ted. 2005. Manufaketure. *The New York Times Magazine.* January 9, 2005. Available at http://query.nytimes.com/gst/fullpage.html?res=9C03E2DD1239F93AA35752C0A9639C8B63.

Forman, Lisa. 2008. "Rights" and wrongs: What utility for the right to health in reforming trade rules on medicines? *Health and Human Rights* 10 (2) (2008): 37. Retrieved on September 13, 2011, from www.hhrjournal.org/index.php/hhr/article/viewArticle/80.

Foucault, Michel. 1978. *The history of sexuality.* 1990 ed. New York: Pantheon Books.

Frank, Richard G., and David S. Salkever. 1997. Generic entry and the pricing of pharmaceuticals. *NBER Working Paper Series* Vol. w5306 (May 1997).

Gauri, Varun, and Daniel M. Brinks. 2008. *Courting social justice: Judicial enforcement of social and economic rights in the developing world.* Cambridge, UK, and New York: Cambridge University Press.

Gerth, Jeff, and Sheryl Gay Stolberg. 2000. Medicine merchants/cultivating alliances; with quiet, unseen ties, drug makers sway debate. *The New York Times,* October 5.

Giron, Erick. 2008. El estado continuará comprando medicinas por contrato abierto *el periódico El Periodico,* June 30, 2008, 2008, sec Pais. Retrieved on July 30, 2011, from www.elperiodico.com.gt/es/20080630/pais/59428.

Glendon, Mary Ann. 2001. *A world made new: Eleanor Roosevelt and the Universal Declaration of Human Rights.* New York: Random House.

———. 2003. The forgotten crucible: The Latin American influence on the universal human rights idea. *Harvard Human Rights Journal* 16: 27.

Global Intellectual Property Center. n/d. *Intellectual property: Creating jobs, saving lives, improving the world.* Washington, DC: U.S. Chamber of Commerce.

Gloppen, Siri, and Mindy Jane Roseman. 2011. Introduction: Can litigation bring justice to health? In *Litigating health rights: Can courts bring more justice to health?,* eds. Siri Gloppen and Alicia Ely Yamin. Cambridge, MA: Harvard University Press.

Godoy, Angelina Snodgrass, and Alejandro Cerón. 2011. Changing drug markets under new intellectual property regimes: The view from Central America. *American Journal of Public Health* 101 (7): 1186.

Goodale, Mark. 2006. Ethical theory as social practice. *American Anthropologist* 108 (1): 25–37.

———. 2007. "Locating rights, envisioning law between the global and the local," introduction to M. Goodale and Sally Engle Merry (eds.), *The practice of human rights: Tracking law between the global and the local*. Cambridge, UK: Cambridge University Press.

Goodman, Zoe. 2007. *Costa Rica: Fortalecimiento de las leyes de patentes, debilitamiento de los derechos humanos. presentación ante el comité de derechos económicos, sociales y culturales*. Geneva: 3D. Retrieved on July 31, 2011, from www.3dthree.org/pdf_3D/3DCDESC_CostaRica.pdf.

Grabowski, Henry G., and Margaret Kyle. 2007. Generic competition and market exclusivity periods in pharmaceuticals. *Managerial and Decision Economics* 28 (4–5): 491–502.

Grandin, Greg. 2004. *The last colonial massacre: Latin America in the cold war*. Chicago: University of Chicago Press. Available at www.loc.gov/catdir/toc/ ecip0415/2004000727.html.

———. 2005. The instruction of great catastrophe: Truth commissions, national history, and state formation in Argentina, Chile, and Guatemala. *American Historical Review* 110 (1) (2): 46–67. Available at http://search.ebscohost .com/login.aspx?direct=true&db=a9h&AN=16273761&site=ehost-live.

Green, Linda Buckley. 1989. Consensus and coercion: Primary health care and the Guatemalan state. *Medical Anthropology Quarterly* 3 (3, The Political Economy of Primary Health Care in Costa Rica, Guatemala, Nicaragua, and El Salvador) (September): 246–257. Available at www.jstor.org/stable/648641.

Gruskin, Sofia, and Daniel Tarantola. 2002. Health and human rights. In *The Oxford textbook of public health*, 4th ed., eds. Roger Detels, James McEwan, Robert Beaglehole, and Heizo Tanaka. Oxford, UK: Oxford University Press.

Hamilton, John. 2005. TLC y genéricos sí coexisten. *Siglo Veintiuno*, January 9.

———. 2011. 05Guatemala659, Guatemala's congress reinstates data protection. March 11, 2005. Wikileaks, Retrieved on August 1, 2011, from http:// wikileaks.org/cable/2005/03/05GUATEMALA659.html.

Hardt, Michael, and Antonio Negri. 2000. *Empire*. Cambridge, MA: Harvard University Press.

Hayden, Cori. 2007. A generic solution? Pharmaceuticals and the politics of the similar in Mexico. *Current Anthropology* 48 (4) (August): 475–495. Available at www.jstor.org/stable/10.1086/518301.

Health GAP. 2005. Transcript: CAFTA and access to essential medicines, July 21 teleconference. Retrieved on July 31, 2011, from www.healthgap.org/camp/trade_docs/transcript.doc.

Heggenhougen, H. K. 1984. Will primary health care efforts be allowed to succeed? *Social Science & Medicine* 19 (3): 217–224.

Helfer, Laurence R. 2007. International rights approaches to intellectual property: Toward a human rights framework for intellectual property. *U.C.Davis Law Review.* 40 (3): 971.

Helfer, Laurence R., and Austin, Graeme W. 2011. *Human rights and intellectual property mapping the global interface.* Cambridge, UK: Cambridge University Press.

Hemminki, Elina, Hanna K. Toiviainen, and Lauri Vuorenkoski. 2010. Cooperation between patient organisations and the drug industry in Finland. *Social Science & Medicine* 70 (8) (4): 1171–1175.

Hernández, David. 2010. Entrevista al viceministro de políticas de salud, Dr. Eduardo Espinoza, sobre el anteproyecto de ley de medicamentos. *Diario CoLatino*, April 6, sec Portada. Retrieved on July 31, 2011, from www.diariocolatino.com/es/20100406/nacionales/78573/?tpl=69.

Hernández-Gonzalez, Greivin, and Max Valverde. 2009. *Evaluación del impacto de las disposiciones de ADPIC + en el mercado institucional de medicamentos de costa rica.* Geneva: International Center for Trade and Sustainable Development, Documento de Fondo No. 26.

Herrling, P. 2007. Patent sense. *Nature* 449 (7159) (September 13): 174–175.

Hestermeyer, Holger. 2007. *Human rights and the WTO: The case of patents and access to medicines.* Oxford, UK: Oxford University Press.

Hogerzeil, Hans V., Melanie Samson, Jaume Vidal Casanovas, and Ladan Rahmani-Ocora. 2006. Is access to essential medicines as part of the fulfilment of the right to health enforceable through the courts? *The Lancet* 368 (9532) (22 July): 305.

Homedes, Nuria, Antonio Ugalde, and Joan Rovira Forns. 2005. The World Bank, pharmaceutical policies, and health reforms in Latin America. *International Journal of Health Services* 35 (4): 691.

Hudson, John. 2000. Generic take-up in the pharmaceutical market following patent expiry: A multi-country study. *International Review of Law and Economics* 20 (2) (6): 205–221.

Hurwitz, Mark A., Richard E. Caves, and Harvard Institute of Economic Research. 1986. *Persuasion or information? Promotion and the shares of brand-name and generic pharmaceuticals.* Cambridge, MA: Harvard Institute of Economic Research.

Jones, Kathryn. 2008. In whose interest? Relationships between health consumer groups and the pharmaceutical industry in the UK. *Sociology of Health & Illness* 30 (6): 929–943.

Kanavos, Panos, Joan Costa-Font, and Elizabeth Seeley. 2008. Competition in off-patent drug markets: Issues, regulation and evidence. *Economic Policy* 23 (55): 499–544.

Kapczynski, Amy. 2009. Harmonization and its discontents: A case study of TRIPS implementation in India's pharmaceutical sector. *California Law Review* 97: 1571–1651.

Keck, Margaret, and Kathryn Sikkink. 1998. *Activists beyond borders: Advocacy networks in international politics.* Ithaca, NY: Cornell University Press.

Kennedy, David. 2004. *The dark sides of virtue: Reassessing international humanitarianism.* Princeton, NJ: Princeton University Press.

Klug, Heinz. 2008. Law, politics, and access to essential medicines in developing countries. *Politics and Society* 36 (2): 207–246.

Kroeger, A., H. Ochoa, B. Arana, A. Diaz, N. Rizzo, and W. Flores. 2001. Inadequate drug advice in the pharmacies of Guatemala and Mexico: The scale of the problem and explanatory factors. *Annals of Tropical Medicine and Parasitology* 95 (6) (September): 605–616.

Kuttner, Robert. 1991. *The end of laissez-faire: National purpose and the global economy after the cold war.* New York: Knopf.

Lake, David A., and Wendy Wong. 2009. The politics of networks: Interests, power, and human rights norms. In *Networked Politics: Agency, Power, and Governance,* Miles Kahler, ed. Ithaca, NY: Cornell University Press.

Lemus, Efren, and Rodrigo Baires Quezada. 2011. Siempre he sido algo insurrecta. *El Faro,* March 9, sec Temas. Retrieved on July 31, 2011, from www.elfaro .net/es/201103/el_agora/3633/?st-cuerpo=0.

Levitt, Peggy, and Sally Merry. 2009. Vernacularization on the ground: Local uses of global women's rights in Peru, China, India and the United States. *Global Networks* 9 (4): 441–461.

Lofgren, Hans. 2004. Pharmaceuticals and the consumer movement: The ambivalences of "patient power." *Australian Health Review* 28: 228.

Love, James. 2009. *Obama administration rules texts of new IPR agreement are state secrets.* Huffington Post. Retrieved on July 26, 2011, from www.huffingtonpost .com/james-love/obama-administration-rule_b_174450.html.

Marroquín Elías, Maria Angela. 2003. *Investigación de los sistemas básicos de salud integral en El Salvador.* San Salvador: Acción para la Salud en El Salvador—APSAL.

Martínez, Gerson Eli, and Alejandra Castro Bonilla. 2008. *Propiedad intelectual y acceso a medicamentos esenciales de calidad en Centroamérica.* San Salvador: FUNDE.

Marx, Karl, and Helen Lederer. 1958. *On the Jewish question.* Cincinnati, OH: Hebrew Union College-Jewish Institute of Religion.

Maupin, Jonathan Nathaniel. 2009. "Fruit of the accords": Healthcare reform and civil participation in highland Guatemala. *Social Science & Medicine* 68 (8) (4): 1456–1463.

Mazer, Roslyn A. 2001, September 30. From T-shirts to terrorism: That fake Nike swoosh may be helping to fund Bin Laden's network. *Washington Post,* sec B.

McCann, Michael W. 1994. *Rights at work: Pay equity reform and the politics of legal mobilization.* Chicago: University of Chicago Press.

Merry, Sally Engle. 2005. Human rights and gender violence: Translating international law into local justice. Chicago: The University of Chicago Press.

Miranda, Jose. n.d. "Una Experiencia De Acción Colectiva En Torno Al Acceso a Medicamentos Esenciales En Guatemala." Unpublished manuscript.

Morales, Lidia. 2004. Educación, salud y tierra: Tres propuestas ante los modelos impulsados por las instituciones financieras internacionales. *Portadores De Sueños: Pensamiento y Acción En Salud* 3 (9) (January–April): 7.

Morgan, Lynn M. 1990. International politics and primary health care in Costa Rica. *Social Science & Medicine* 30 (2): 211–219.

Moss, Giles D. 2007. *Pharmaceuticals—Where's the brand logic? Branding lessons and strategies.* Binghamton, NY: Haworth Press.

Mutua, Makau. 2002. *Human rights: A political and cultural critique.* Philadelphia: University of Pennsylvania Press.

Nelson, Paul, and Ellen Dorsey. 2003. At the nexus of human rights and development: New methods and strategies of global NGOs. *World Development* 31(12): 2013–2026.

Norheim, Ole Frithjof, and Siri Gloppen. 2011. Litigating for medicines: How can we assess impact on health outcomes? In *Litigating health rights: Can courts bring more justice to health?*, eds. Alicia Ely Yamin and Siri Gloppen, 304–332. Cambridge, MA: Harvard University Press.

Norheim, Ole Frithjof, and Bruce Wilson. 2010. "Health rights litigation and access to medicines: Priority classification of successful cases from Costa Rica's constitutional chamber of the supreme court." Unpublished paper presented at the May 2010 Meetings of the Law and Society Association in Chicago, Illinois.

Organizacion Panamericana de la Salud. 2005. *Opinion tecnica al evento DNCAE no. 08-2005 para la provisión de productos medicinales y farmaceúticos paquete I, II, y III.* Organizacion Panamericana de la Salud, Expediente No. EIO.GUA 442-2004/DESC.

Oxfam America. 2007. *All costs, no benefits: How TRIPS-plus intellectual property rules in the US–Jordan FTA affect access to medicines.* Washington, DC: Oxfam America.

Palmer, Steven. 2005. Esbozo histórico de la medicina estatal en américa central. *Dynamis* 25: 59.

Pan American Health Organization. 2007. *Health systems profile of Guatemala.* Washington, DC: PAHO.

Paugh, Wayne. 2008. World intellectual property day & beyond: How the U.S. government, private sector, and academia support international outreach on intellectual property rights. Paper presented at Foreign Press Center briefing, Washington DC. Retrieved on July 26, 2011, from http://2002-2009-fpc .state.gov/103962.htm.

Perehudoff, S. Katrina, and Teresa Leonardo Alves. 2011. *The patient and consumer voice and pharmaceutical industry sponsorship.* Amsterdam, Netherlands: Health Action International (HAI) Europe. Retrieved on September 15, 2011, from http://haieurope.org/publications/reports/.

Power, Timothy J., and Jennifer M. Cyr. 2009. Mapping political legitimacy in Latin America. *International Social Science Journal* 60 (196): 253–272.

Reiffen, David, and Michael R. Ward. 2006. "Generic drug industry dynamics," *The Review of Economics and Statistics* 87 (1): 37–49.

Robinson, William I. 1996. *Promoting polyarchy: Globalization, US intervention, and hegemony.* Cambridge, UK: Cambridge University Press.

———. 2003. *Transnational conflicts: Central America, social change, and globalization.* New York and London: Verso.

———. 2004. *A theory of global capitalism: Production, class, and state in a transnational world.* Baltimore, MD: Johns Hopkins University Press.

Romero, J., E. Muñoz, and C. Vidal. 1975. Evolution of teaching of preventive and social medicine in Latin America. *Revista Médica de Chile* 103 (9): 628–633.

Rosenberg, Gerald. 1991. *The hollow hope: Can courts bring about social change?* Chicago: University of Chicago Press

Rovira, Joan, Ismail Abbas, and Miguel Cortés. 2009. *Guide to the IPRIA (intellectual property rights impact aggregate) model.* Geneva: International Center for Trade and Sustainable Development. Retrieved on July 27, 2011, from ictsd.org/downloads/2010/03/guide-to-the-ipria-model.pdf.

Ruhl, J. Mark. 2011. Political corruption in Central America: Assessment and explanation. *Latin American Politics and Society* 53 (1): 33–58.

Santos, Boaventura de Sousa. 2002. Toward a multicultural conception of human rights. *Beyond Law* 9 (25), June 2002: 9–32.

———. 2005. Beyond neoliberal governance: The world social forum as subaltern cosmopolitan politics and legality. In *Law and globalization from below: Towards a cosmopolitan legality*, eds. Boaventura de Sousa Santos and César A. Rodríguez Garavito, 29–63. Cambridge, UK: Cambridge University Press.

Scheingold, Stuart. 1974. *The politics of rights: Lawyers, public policy, and political change*. New Haven, CT: Yale University Press.

Schuftan, Claudio. 2007. A guided tour through key principles and issues of the human rights–based framework as applied to health. *Social Medicine* 2(2): 68–78.

Scott Morton, Fiona M. 2000. Barriers to entry, brand advertising, and generic entry in the US pharmaceutical industry. *International Journal of Industrial Organization* 18 (7) (10): 1085–1104.

Sell, Susan K. 2003. *Private power, public law: The globalization of intellectual property rights*. Cambridge studies in international relations. Vol. 88. Cambridge, UK, and New York: Cambridge University Press. Available at www .loc.gov/catdir/description/cam031/2002035020.html and www.loc.gov/catdir/ toc/cam031/2002035020.html.

———. 2010. The global IP upward ratchet, anti-counterfeiting and piracy enforcement efforts: The state of play. *PIJIP Research Paper no. 15*. 15. Retrieved on July 27, 2011, from http://digitalcommons.wcl.american.edu/research/15/.

Sell, Susan K., and Aseem Prakash. 2004. Using ideas strategically: The contest between business and NGO networks in intellectual property rights. *International Studies Quarterly* 48 (1): 143–175.

Shadlen, Ken. 2009. The politics of patents and drugs in Brazil and Mexico: The industrial bases of health policies. *Comparative Politics* 42 (1).

Shaffer, Ellen, and Joseph Brenner. 2009. A trade agreement's impact on access to generic drugs. *Health Affairs* 28 (5).

Shaffer, Ellen, Joseph Brenner, and Shayna Lewis. 2009. CAFTA: Barriers to access in medicines in Guatemala. *Health and Human Rights Open Forum*. Retrieved on July 17, 2012, from www.hhrjournal.org/index.php/hhr/article/viewFile/ 246/363.

Sklair, Leslie. 2000. *The transnational capitalist class*. Oxford: Wiley-Blackwell.

Smith-Nonini, Sandra C. 1997. "Popular" health and the state: Dialectics of the peace process in El Salvador. *Social Science & Medicine* 44 (5) (3): 635–345.

———. 2010. *Healing the body politic: El Salvador's popular struggle for health rights—from civil war to neoliberal peace.* Studies in medical anthropology. New Brunswick, NJ: Rutgers University Press.

Spalding, Rose. 2007. Civil society engagement in trade negotiations: CAFTA opposition movements in El Salvador. *Latin American Politics & Society* 49 (4): 85.

Stiglitz, Joseph E. 2006. *Making globalization work.* New York: W. W. Norton & Co. Available at www.loc.gov/catdir/toc/ecip0616/2006020633.html.

Tajer, Debora. 2003. Latin American social medicine: Roots, development during the 1990s, and current challenges. *American Journal of Public Health* 93 (12) (December 1): 2023–2027.

Tushnet, Mark. 1984. A critique of rights: An essay on rights. *Texas Law Review* 62 (May 1984): 1363.

UNAIDS. 2007. *AIDS epidemic update: Global summary.* Geneva: UNAIDS.

———. 2010. *Global report: UNAIDS report on the global aids epidemic 2010.* Geneva: UNAIDS.

U.S. Army Information School, Carlisle Barracks, Pa. 1946. *Pillars of peace. documents pertaining to American interest in establishing a lasting world peace, January 1941–February 1946.* Carlisle Barracks, PA: Book Dept., Army Information School.

U.S. Food and Drug Administration. 2003. *Improving innovation in medical technology: Beyond 2002.* Rockville, MD: FDA.

U.S. Government Accountability Office. 2006. *New drug development science, business, regulatory, and intellectual property issues cited as hampering drug development efforts: Report to congressional requesters.* In U.S. Government Accountability Office [database online]. [Washington, D.C.]. Retrieved on January 3, 2013, from www.gao.gov/new.items/d0749.pdf.

Vargas Ayala, Cesar Humberto. 2006. Consecuencias jurídicas en materia de la ley de propiedad intelectual sobre comercialización y distribución de medicamentos genéricos frente a la ratificación del DR-CAFTA por parte de guatemala. Licenciado en Ciencias Jurídicas y Sociales, Guatemala City: Universidad de San Carlos de Guatemala, Facultad de Ciencias Jurídicas y Sociales.

Villegas de Olazával, Hugo. 2006. Atención primaria en salud: Escenarios, renovación, desafíos. *Gaceta Médica De Costa Rica* 2.

Waitzkin, H., C. Iriart, A. Estrada, and S. Lamadrid. 2001a. Social medicine in Latin America: Productivity and dangers facing the major national groups. *Lancet* 358 (9278) (July 28): 315–323.

———. 2001b. Social medicine then and now: Lessons from Latin America. *American Journal of Public Health* 91 (10) (October): 1592–1601.

Weissman, Robert. 2008. Cheaper drugs are as important as improved health infrastructure. *The New Times (Kigali)*, May 6.

Wilson, Bruce. 2011. "Costa Rica health rights litigation: Causes and consequences." In *Litigating health rights: Can courts bring more justice to health?*, eds. Alicia Ely Yamin and Siri Gloppen, 132–154. Cambridge, MA: Harvard University Press.

Wilson, Richard. 2006. "Afterword to 'Anthropology and human rights in a new key': The social life of human rights." *American Anthropologist* 108 (1): 77–83.

World Health Organization. 2005. WHO model list of essential medicines, 14th ed., in World Health Organization [database online]. Geneva: WHO. Retrieved on July 30, 2011, from http://whqlibdoc.who.int/hq/2005/a87017_eng.pdf.

———. 2010. WHO statistical information system, in World Health Organization [database online]. Retrieved on July 24, 2011, from http://apps.who.int/whosis/data/Search.jsp.

Wright-Carozza, Paolo. 2003. From conquest to constitutions: Retrieving a Latin American tradition of the idea of human rights. *Human Rights Quarterly* 25 (2): 281.

Yamin, Alicia Ely. 2010. Shades of dignity: Exploring the demands of equality in applying human rights frameworks to health. *Health and Human Rights: An International Journal* 11 (2). Available at www.hhrjournal.org/index.php/hhr/article/view/169.

———. 2011. "Power, suffering, and courts: Reflections on promoting health rights through judicialization," in *Litigating health rights: Can courts bring more justice to health?*, 333–372. Cambridge, MA: Human Rights Program, Harvard Law School, Harvard University Press.

Yamin, Alicia Ely, and Siri Gloppen, eds. 2011. *Litigating health rights: Can courts bring more justice to health?* Cambridge, MA: Human Rights Program, Harvard Law School; Harvard University Press.

Zarembo, Alan. 1999. Life-or-death lottery. *Newsweek (Atlantic Edition)* 134 (1) (July 5): 25. Available at http://search.ebscohost.com/login.aspx?direct=true&db=f5h&AN=1998561&site=ehost-live.

Index

Gerth, Jeff, 124
Gillespie-White, Lee, 25
Girón, Erik, 73
Glendon, Mary Ann, 33, 35, 56
globalization, 135–42; global class for-
    mation, 137, 157n7; human rights
    issues regarding, 13, 14, 16, 19, 23, 37,
    38, 41, 48–49, 131, 141–42, 150; and
    the state, 136–37; Washington Con-
    sensus, 29, 157n8. *See also* markets
Gloppen, Siri, 108, 110, 117–18, 126
González Torres, Víctor, 93
Goodale, Mark: on global/local dichot-
    omy, 105; on human rights, 12, 105
Goodman, Zoe, 94
Grabowski, Henry G., 23
Grandin, Greg, 56, 133, 157nn1,3
Green, Linda Buckley, 82
Gruskin, Sofia, 39
Guatemala: access litigation in, 17–19,
    108, 109–21, 122–25, 144, 156n4; ac-
    cess to antiretroviral therapy in, 54,
    55; and CAFTA, 1–2, 3, 46, 61–62, 63,
    80, 85, 86, 87–92, 94, 101, 126; cardio-
    vascular diseases in, 54; civil war in,
    2, 3, 83, 111; clinical trials in, 154n1;
    Clínica Luis Ángel Garcia, 51–52;
    Constitution, 113, 120; Constitutional
    Court, 113, 119–20, 121, 126–27,
    156n4; corruption in, 112, 123–24,
    125; coup of 1954, 3; drug prices in,
    66–67; drug regulations in, 68–69,
    118, 122, 123; generics industry in, 17,
    59, 90, 91, 92, 155n11; Guatecompras,
    57–58; health code of, 113; Heroes of
    Hope, 107–8, 110; HIV/AIDS in, 1, 4,
    46, 51–52, 72–73, 115, 117, 138; hu-
    man rights ombudsman (PDH), 72,
    110, 112, 113, 121, 122, 123, 132; infant
    mortality in, 54, 154n1; institutional
    drug purchases in, 57–58, 72–74, 75,
    116; Integrated System for Health
    Attention/Coverage Extension, 84;
    IP in, 9, 59, 61–62, 63, 72–75, 76–77,
    80, 87–92, 94, 101, 138, 154n5; justice
    system, 111–21, 122, 126–28, 144,

156n4; Kaletra purchased by, 72–74,
    75, 77, 155n12; life expectancy at birth
    in, 54, 154n1; malnutrition in, 53;
    maternal mortality rates in, 53; Maya
    in, 2, 3; Ministry of Health, 57, 91;
    Nexium purchased by, 74, 77; patent
    laws in, 18, 61, 62, 88, 92, 127; patients'
    associations in, 107–8, 110, 112, 113,
    121, 122–23, 124–25, 132; per capital
    government expenditure on health
    in, 54, 57; primary health care in, 83;
    relations with United States, 90–91,
    138; resistance to CAFTA in, 85,
    87–92, 101; Social Security Institute
    (IGSS), 18, 57, 90, 113–14, 117, 118–20,
    121, 122–24, 125, 156n5; social se-
    curity system in, 56, 57, 113–14, 115,
    116, 118–20, 122–24, 154n3, 156n5;
    test data protection laws in, 59, 61, 63,
    66–67, 74, 76–77, 88, 89–91, 92; TRIPS
    implementation in, 59; UN Mission
    in, 2
Guevara, Giovanni, 70, 98, 99

Hamilton, John, 89–91
Hardt, Michael, 138, 140
Harvard Institute of Economic Research,
    67
Hayden, Cori, 69
Health Action International (HAI), 71,
    99
Health GAP, 41, 88, 94
Heggenbougen, H. K., 83
Helfer, Laurence R., 130, 131
Hemminki, Elina, 124
Herceptin, 117, 121
Hernández, David, 97
Hernández-González, Greivin, 64
Herrling, P., 41
Hestermeyer, Holger, 27
HIV/AIDS, 39, 158n10; in Guatemala, 1,
    4, 46, 51–52, 72–73, 115, 117, 138; in
    South Africa, 7, 42. *See also* antiretro-
    viral drugs
Hogerzeil, Hans V., 6, 108, 110, 120
Homedes, Nuria, 31, 83

Printed and bound by CPI Group (UK) Ltd, Croydon, CR0 4YY

23/04/2025

14660937-0001